NORMS FOR THE NOVEL

NORMS
FOR THE NOVEL

Harold C. Gardiner, S.J.

LITERARY EDITOR OF
AMERICA

Revised Edition

HANOVER HOUSE
A DIVISION OF DOUBLEDAY & COMPANY, INC.
GARDEN CITY, NEW YORK
1960

Nihil Obstat: MYLES M. BOURKE, S.T.D.
Imprimatur: ✠ FRANCIS CARDINAL SPELLMAN
             Archbishop of New York
             November 16, 1959

The *nihil obstat* and *imprimatur* are official declarations that a book or pamphlet is free of doctrinal or moral error. No implication is contained therein that those who have granted the *nihil obstat* and *imprimatur* agree with the contents, opinions or statements expressed.

808.3
Grar

ACKNOWLEDGMENTS

Selections from *The Dynamics of Literature* by Nathan Comfort Starr which appear on pages 55 and 158–59 are used by permission of Columbia University Press, and are copyright 1945 by Columbia University Press.

Selections from the preface of *The Withered Branch: Six Studies in the Modern Novel* by D. S. Savage which appear on pages 126–27 are used by permission of Farrar, Straus & Cudahy, Inc.

Selections from *On Literature Today* by Van Wyck Brooks which appear on pages 119–20 are reprinted by permission of E. P. Dutton & Co., Inc., and are copyright 1941 by Van Wyck Brooks.

Contents

FOREWORD

WHEN an author is preparing a second edition of one of his works, he finds himself, I would imagine (for this is the first time I have had such a happy fate thrust upon me), of two minds. He is amazed that the first edition attracted so much attention that a second is now called for; he is inclined to be smug and wonder why the original publisher did not print enough copies in the first place to satisfy the clamoring audience which has had to be told that the first edition is out of print and that it will simply have to possess its soul in whatever patience it can summon up.

But seriously, since the America Press published *Norms for the Novel* in 1953, the entire edition has been truly exhausted and there had been a continuing demand for the book. Also, there have been repeated requests to bring it up to date by the inclusion and consideration of books published since it was originally issued. I was delighted to be able to comply with these many requests when Hanover House approached me with the suggestion that a revised and updated edition of *Norms for the Novel* be prepared for publication.

These are the extrinsic reasons for the preparation of the second edition. That this small essay at the restatement of some critical principles for criticism of the novel has some intrinsic value was suggested originally, and is still hinted at, by the continuing publication of books which state the problems that face the contemporary novelist. Such books, to mention a few, are *Spiritual Problems in Contemporary Literature*, edited by Stanley Romaine Hopper (Harper, 1952), *The Writer in America*, by Van Wyck Brooks (Dutton, 1953), *Modern Literature and the Religious Frontier*, by Nathan A.

9

Scott, Jr. (Harper, 1958), and *The Prophetic Voice in Modern Fiction*, by William R. Mueller (Association Press, 1959). In these books, and in many others that might be cited, there is a frank and almost explicit admission that too much of the criticism of the novel in our recent past has been based on the assumption that a novel is simply a sociological tract dressed up a bit in fictional trapping. The sociological novel is still with us, of course. But it would seem that the current has set in and is running more strongly every day toward the creation of fiction that is facing up more squarely to the existence in man of more than social problems, strains and imbalances. Once the novelist faces that "more," he begins to show (as Hannah Arendt pointed out in the Summer, 1949, issue of *The Kenyon Review*) "a conspicuous and curious affinity with poetry on the one hand and philosophy on the other." Such an affinity becomes more and more evident in the work of such a novelist as Robert Penn Warren, who is at once a poet and a "philosophical" searcher. His work will be referred to later in this book.

The affinity is certainly conspicuous, but it is really not so curious, for once the novelist strives to get behind the social façade of human behavior, he is ineluctably plunged into the ultimate "whys" of human action; once he strives to give an honest and convincing answer to these, he is treading on moral grounds. Once he treads there, he is involved in a religious "engagement," as the French love—and rightly—to say.

If the novelist's approach, then, has been undergoing this heartening permutation here in America (following at some remove a kindred change on the Continent), it would seem that critical principles for the judgment of the American novel might well reflect on the values that the novelist is now somewhat tardily facing.

That is the justification of the following study. It tries to put before critic and reader of the modern novel two sets of principles in the form of propositions which I hope have not been oversimplified in an attempt at clarity. The first set of principles attempts to answer the question: Do the norms of morality have any bearing on the novelist's art, and if so, what bearing? The second set of principles faces the question: Granting that these moral norms do have a place in the novelist's art, what is that art designed to achieve? Throughout, as I remark in the body of the discussion, I have prescinded from the matter of style. We are discussing simply *what* is in a novel —what morally and what artistically—and not *how* that *what* is handled.

This second edition has been brought up to date by the inclusion of books published since 1953, and two sections have been considerably expanded. There has been no change, obviously, in the basic principles.

I may claim in all modesty that the original *Norms for the Novel* did stimulate thought and discussion, whether or not its conclusions always won total agreement. My obvious hope is that the second edition will be even more widely discussed and that through the discussion readers and teachers will come to see more clearly and deeply the function and the rewards of creative writing and reading.

HAROLD C. GARDINER, S.J.

Campion House,
New York, New York
August 15, 1959

The Background

SINCE this book has grown gradually as a result of controversy and discussion caused by various reviews of mine of novels in the columns of *America*, it may be useful to recount the labyrinths through which the controversy has wound.

The first reviews to provoke demurrers were of books widely discussed at the time—in the early forties. In fact, one of the novels, Betty Smith's *A Tree Grows in Brooklyn*, seems to have been blessed with that bloom of perennial youth which is one of the distinguishing marks of a "classic." The second review took up a book which did not have that cachet; it was, however, the work of an author who seems in some circles to be considered a classic writer, and indeed, if his total output is taken into consideration, his stature is impressive. The book was Sholem Asch's *The Apostle*.

Here are the two reviews, reprinted in their entirety. The first was published in *America* for August 21, 1943, the second in the issue of September 18, 1943. Of *A Tree Grows in Brooklyn*, I wrote:

> You may not know it, but there is a Society for the Prevention of Disparaging Remarks about Brooklyn. Its President reports that slurs against that noble Borough dropped from 6,457 in 1941 to 2,623 in 1942. I venture to state that when this book becomes well-known, as it certainly will, slurs against Brooklyn will be greatly counterbalanced by encomia heaped upon her, or at least upon this one citizen, Betty Smith, and the family of which she writes.
>
> For this is a remarkably fresh and warmly humane story. It is

called a novel; it is rather the biography of Francie Nolan, from her twelfth to her sixteenth year. The first chapter opens with her taking her weekly collection of junk to Cheap Charlie's, to collect her fabulous penny; the last chapter closes with her ready to move from the old neighborhood and start in college. In between, adolescent dreams and impressions, escapades, dangers and disappointments are set before us in a fresh simplicity of style and language that is truly good.

Francie is Irish, Catholic and poor. Irish readers may not like the book, but they ought not forget that the slovenly characters in it are more than overbalanced by the warm-hearted goodness and generosity that animate the others. The Catholic elements in the story are a little clumsily handled at times, with the consequent suspicion that the author is not quite sure whether the beliefs are motivated by faith or superstition. Emphasis on poverty—which, of course, cannot be avoided, for that is the environment the author has chosen—tends to stress the impression that poverty of itself is brutal. Francie was poor, her life was hard and "under-privileged," but she had a marvelous mother, a kind, companionable (if too frequently drunk) father, a warm, loyal family life—and lots of fun. If that be brutality, plenty of children could stand a bit of it.

One or two incidents in the story could well have been played down a little, as, for example, Francie's nearly disastrous experience with a pervert; but these frank passages and the vulgarity of expression that crops up from time to time need not be a worry to sensible and mature readers.

These elements, of course, follow from the fact that the author chose to put her foot in this particular portion of the stream; granting that she writes of that type of life in that town at that time, the picture is authentic. Certainly we have in this alive book a vivid recapturing of childhood. Any reader who ever collected old newspapers in his youth, under the impression that he would soon get rich thereby, who fell in love with vaudeville stars, who reached seventh heaven with a penny bag of cake-ends from the neighborhood bakery, will see his youth again, and nostalgically, in this Brooklyn masterpiece.

This was my judgment of Sholem Asch's *The Apostle:*

Storms, I am afraid, will blow up over this book, as they did over the author's earlier *The Nazarene,* and it will be good to get the storm-signals out early. Catholics will definitely have to be on their guard, for the reverence for Our Divine Lord which saved them from being taken in by Asch's reconstruction of His life in *The Nazarene* will not be so strong a safeguard against the falsity of this picture of Saint Paul and the early Church.

That is the story of the book: it is the life and labors of Saint Paul. Let it be said in all fairness that it is a monumental book, and strangely attractive, for the tremendous events are real and moving in Asch's biblically-flavored style. The author is a scholar, in the sense that he knows the period and the customs (compare him for depth in this with Lloyd Douglas' knowledge as shown in *The Robe*) and shows wide acquaintance with Saint Paul's Epistles, in the phrases of which much of the story is told (though not, of course, in the Catholic version).

But alas! there his scholarship ends, for he has no insight into the real meaning of either Saint Paul's life or the Church. The main core of difficulty lies in the question of the Judaizers in the early Church—those early Christians who wanted still, after conversion, to follow the Law in all details, and demanded that the converted Gentiles be made to do the same. Catholic teaching is that the difficulty was officially resolved at the first Council of the Church, held at Jerusalem, and Saint Peter and Saint Paul, though they did differ for a time in the matter of practical application, agreed on the dogma. The author, however, who seems to be infected with the rationalism of some of the higher critics like Bauer, would hold, I think, a dual primitive Christianity, Paulinism and Petrinism, instead of the one Christianity established by its Divine Founder.

Indeed, the Divinity of the Messiah is doubtful in the extreme in the pages of this book. Christ is referred to, true, as the Son of God, as one who sat at the right hand of the Father before creation, but when we read "the apostle Paul begins to find his way back to God, Whom he had for a time lost, because of his love for the Messiah . . ." the titles mean nothing. Again, especially in the later portions of the book, Saint Peter does not understand the "special doctrine" of Saint Paul about the Messiah; evidently Saint Paul is the one who has foisted the Divinity of Christ on the Church; indeed, that Church was founded by the Apostle.

There are other errors that vitiate the historicity of the story: it was the Romans, not the Jews, who crucified Christ; our Lady, who is also the mother of Saint James, is an old, broken woman when the story starts; Baptism is conferred in the name of the Messiah, not under the Trinitarian formula; the Eucharist is only a commemorative meal. Saint Paul's visions are so described as to make them seem very like epileptic fits.

The aim and purpose of the book seem to be summed up in the epilog. There Asch gives thanks that God has strengthened him to write this book and *The Nazarene*, "which are one work, so that I might set forth in them the merit of Israel, whom Thou hast elected to bring the light of the faith to the nations of the world, for Thy glory and out of Thy love of mankind."

That is a reverent purpose; only, it is historically false. Israel has lost its Messianic function; it bears no light, but it and all other tribes and nations and peoples have now but one source of light, Jesus Christ, the Son of God, working through His Church, which is not the synagogue.

These two reviews, then, gave the start to what developed into a vigorous controversy. This was waged largely in the correspondence columns of *America*, though many of the letters pro and con did not find space for publication. Not a few of the letters made it almost impossible to decline the controversy, since they called into question not only the reviewer's competence, but constituted an almost direct charge that *America*'s approach to the whole question of modern fiction was a betrayal of the apostolic nature of Catholic journalism. One such charge, for instance, averred that the review of the Asch book had practically "farmed out" *America*'s columns to *PM* (the pinkish

New York daily that has since ceased publication) and to *The Protestant* (a belligerently anti-Catholic journal), because the review had "adroitly boosted Asch and damned Lloyd Douglas' *The Robe*." Other correspondents were aghast that *America* could "recommend" such a "filthy" book as *A Tree Grows in Brooklyn*.

A response to these charges was attempted in four articles in *America* (November 20, November 27, December 11, 1943; January 8, 1944), where the effort was made not merely to refute, but to broaden the discussion into a consideration of some moral principles to be used in literary criticism and in constructive reading. These articles were later collected and published in 1944 as a booklet, called *Tenets for Reviewers*. Subsequent editions of this, up to 1952, were slightly expanded and retitled *Tenets for Readers and Reviewers*. Meanwhile the realization was being borne in upon me that a great deal of the difficulty readers, and particularly Catholic readers, experience in making up their mind about the moral tone of much current fiction springs from a misconception of the nature and role of realism in literature. Accordingly, in a series of articles in *America* (December 10, December 17, 1949; January 21, March 18, 1950), I tried to outline what I believe is a distinction about realism that is necessary but commonly overlooked by critics and unrealized by readers. These four articles are included in the present work, as they have their place in rounding out our tentative principles for moral valuation.

How necessary this analysis of realism is became even clearer through much of the reaction to Graham Greene's *The End of the Affair*. Since that novel is used in this work to illustrate many of the principles formulated, it may be helpful to reproduce two articles on Greene which appeared in *America*. The first article (October 27, 1951) ran:

If for no other reason, Graham Greene will have a permanent niche in the history of English literature—and particularly of

Catholic literature—because he manages to write provocative and controversial novels. But the controversy that swirled around *The Power and the Glory* (*The Labyrinthine Ways*) and *The Heart of the Matter* will sound like a muted murmur compared with the storms that will thunder around his latest book, *The End of the Affair*. I feel that the book demands rather extended treatment, both for its intrinsic importance and to forestall criticism that gets off on the wrong foot.

Perhaps the best way to start is to quote from a very perceptive article on Greene (by Edward Sackville-West in the *Month*, London, September, 1951). It is called "The Electric Hare— Some Aspects of Graham Greene," and is largely a review of Greene's volume of essays, *The Lost Childhood*. Says the author: "Every page of this book is saturated in the belief that original sin is the most important fact about human beings." Now the point is, for a judgment of Greene, not precisely whether this is theologically true or not—for certainly the *fact* of sanctifying grace is equally important—but whether it is actually Greene's view. I believe it is, and I believe that it explains the eschatological tone of all his work. He is not interested, so to say, in the mere problem of good and evil, of sin and virtue, as worked out in *this* situation, by *these* characters. His attention is constantly turned to the ultimate end of *this* situation, of *these* actions— he writes always in terms of heaven and hell.

That is what makes his books, to many tastes, so grim and dour. But that they are Catholic, in the sense that they have as theme some of the great truths of Christian revelation, I believe cannot fairly be doubted. Whether or not those truths are couched in terms that find acceptance on grounds of propriety and so on is another matter.

That will be the crucial point of criticism of *The End of the Affair*. What Greene is saying in this story is as eternally true as much of what St. Augustine said in his *Confessions*, for the burden of the tale is that God is the often unthought-of but ever-present finality of all loves. Even illegitimate love is a blind, fumbling, misdirected search for God. How Greene says this will very probably—and with a lot of justification—be disliked.

18

The story of the book is simple. The title tells it, really. An adultery that has been carried on for years comes to an end, because in the London blitz, the woman, fearing that her lover has been killed in an air-raid, promises God—in whom she really does not believe—that she will end the affair if he is given life. He lives and she—living up to her nebulous idea of obligation—finds herself drawn to the Church and to holiness (it turns out that she had been baptized as a young child). After her early death, a number of apparently miraculous cures seem to be due to her intercession. The man in the affair (who is the narrator of the story) had been even more a disbeliever than the woman, but when his tale ends, he has come to the point where he can at least think that he hates God, who has stepped in to end the affair. Hatred, Greene seems to be saying, argues belief—an echo of the biblical "neither hot nor cold."

So much for the plot. However, I must admit that much of Greene's language is a stumbling-block even to what we have to call a mature reader. It must be remembered in all fairness that the story is told by a long-term lecher. His phrases—objectively blasphemous at times—are his own and fit his character, but they are such that the book is by no means to be commended to the attention of all. It is a shame and could have been avoided by a different narrative device.

Evelyn Waugh, reviewing the book in the same issue of the London *Month* referred to above, says: "*The End of the Affair* is addressed to the Gentiles. It shows them the Church as something in their midst, mysterious and triumphant and working for their good." That, I feel, is true, but the book will also be read by Catholics who are not accustomed to having the Church referred to in terms that spring from a philanderer's mind. That is the ultimate novelistic problem of this controversial book—how can profound spiritual truth (which Greene touches) be told in terms of stark realism? I wish I knew the answer. Until it is a little clearer than at present, I would say that *The End of the Affair* is definitely for the perusal of those professionally interested in the study of the novel.

The second article (December 15, 1951) was as follows:

The time for temporizing is over, it seems. The original notice given to *The End of the Affair* was rather in the form of an interim report, and was not decisive enough to satisfy either myself or the many who have written in to ask "what gave?" Further, it is worth while expending some second thoughts on Graham Greene's latest book, I believe, because he is an extraordinary phenomenon in the world of letters. In modern times there has never been an author so uncompromisingly Catholic in his statements who is at the same time admittedly—by Catholic and non-Catholic critics alike—one of the very greatest living novelists.

His work is, then, something of a touchstone for criticism. If Catholic critics, above all, get him wrong; if they demand from him what they cannot justly seek; if they miss what he is valiantly saying, they will be both unfair to Greene and false to themselves.

What, accordingly, will second thought reveal? Perhaps I can best start by adverting to some critical opinions that seem to me to stress the wrong emphasis in their judgment of *The End of the Affair*. Riley Hughes, for instance, writing in *Best Sellers* for November 15, 1951, thinks that the images of evil are so vivid and tangible (as it were), while the images of good are so "unclothed in the novelist's skill," that "sense wins out over spirit." I believe that I delivered much the same verdict when I wrote that the "profound spiritual truths" of the book were couched in "terms of stark realism." I would like to withdraw my own version while commenting on Mr. Hughes'.

The images of evil *are* more vivid than the images of good—but how can that be otherwise, particularly when the evil wears the trappings of sensuality? It is the drear heritage of our fallen nature that things of sense are more immediately alluring than things of the spirit. Human love is, in a sense, easier to grasp and understand and enjoy than the love of God. And so, it is to make a psychologically unfair and impossible demand of Greene to ask him to make the woman's struggles toward belief in God and love of Him as charged with the immediacy and urgency of actual experience as were the passionate meetings of the lovers.

But that is not the whole gist of the matter. Actually, one of the triumphs of the book, as I see it, lies precisely in the growth depicted in Sarah. It is an interesting and key fact that once the reader turns, with the narrator, to the pages of the diary in which Sarah recounts her agony to be true to her promise to end the affair, the sensuousness of the language progressively gives way to a reflected and filtered treatment of passion that removes even the slightest suspicion of undue preoccupation with sense at the expense of spirit. As Sarah's realization of real love and purity grows, Greene's style mirrors the purity of her new-found world.

But in so doing, Greene achieves the further remarkable feat of keeping the character true to herself. She does not become, at one leap, a tinsel saint, basking securely in the love of God. She is still the passionate woman, she still feels the imperious call of the flesh. And here I cannot refrain from remarking (perhaps annoyingly, for the comparison is somewhat overworked) how inevitably Greene recalls St. Augustine to mind.

One of the marvels of that great saint's *Confessions* lies precisely here—the humble frankness with which he depicts himself after his conversion as still the same passionate man. But he is now the passionate man who can ask:

> But what is it that I love when I love You? Not the beauty of any bodily thing, nor the order of the seasons, nor the brightness of light that rejoices the eye, nor the sweet melodies of all songs, nor the sweet fragrance of flowers and ointments and spices: not manna nor honey, nor the limbs that carnal love embraces. Yet in a sense I do love light and melody and fragrance and food and embrace when I love my God—the light and the voice and the fragrance and the food and the embrace in the soul, when that light shines upon my soul which no place can contain, that voice sounds which no time can take from me, I breathe that fragrance which no wind scatters, I eat that food which is not lessened by eating, and I lie in that embrace which satiety never comes to sunder. That is what I love, when I love my God. (The version is that of F. J. Sheed.)

If this is not the exact tone that runs through the diary of Sarah, and if it is not a testimony, not that "sense wins out over spirit," but that sense, still being sense, can reflect the beauty of spirit, then I have misread both Augustine and Greene.

This leads immediately, I think, into another criticism leveled at Greene which I conceive to be unfounded. Martin Turnell, the English Catholic critic, writing in the *Commonweal* (October 26, 1951) on "The Religious Novel," calls both Mauriac and Greene to task. "It is impossible," he states, "not to be struck by the vast place occupied by hate and the tiny place reserved for charity in the work of contemporary Catholic novelists. . . . That is the crucial point. They seek not the good points, the redeeming features of their neighbors, but something that will give *the right to hate*."

However this castigation may apply to Mauriac, I believe that it is utterly false of Greene. The judgment, it would appear, springs from a confusion between characters who hate and the *author* who hates. It is true that Greene does portray (though much less frequently than Mauriac) characters ridden by some type of hatred, whether for themselves and their environment (like the priest in *The Power and the Glory* or Scobie in *The Heart of the Matter*) or for someone else (like Bendrix in the present novel). But that is not to say that the author himself is exercising "the right to hate."

In fact, it is pretty hard to discover that Greene hates *anything* in his novels. For one thing, the very objectivity of his portrayal of sin has struck many a Catholic critic (unreasonably, I think) as being a sort of tacit condonation. And so far from hating the characters he creates, Greene's most moving characteristic is a deep compassion and understanding. The best one-sentence summary of Greene I know of is given by one of his own characters. When Bendrix, in *The End of the Affair*, hating (he thinks) Sarah's memory and desiring to hurt her through her husband Henry, blurts out the whole sordid story to Henry before Fr. Crompton, Henry, embarrassed for his guest, says to the priest, "I'm sorry, Father." "You don't need to be," said the priest. "I know when a man's in pain."

Graham Greene knows when a man's in pain. The pain most of his characters are in is the pain of loss or of lack. The significant forward step in *The End of the Affair* is that one character, at least, stands at last horrified at the edge of the chasm and through God's grace goes about filling it with God's grace. "I might have taken a lifetime spending a little love at a time, doling it out here and there, on this man and that," says Sarah. "But even the first time . . . we spent all we had. You were there, teaching us to squander . . . so that one day we might have nothing left except this love of You."

Surprisingly enough, it was the slick and sophisticated *New Yorker* (in a review by Anthony West, November 10, 1951) that caught most clearly this positive facet of Greene's latest novel. "The negative aspects of belief," says Mr. West, "have gone into the discard." Unfortunately, in trying to show how different from Greene's earlier novels *The End of the Affair* is, the critic builds up a largely fictitious case against *Brighton Rock*, *The Power and the Glory* and *The Heart of the Matter*. In all three, we are told, the pivotal point is that the protagonist is undone

> by contact with female flesh. . . . It is this fear of life and creativity taking the form of fear of woman, so often found in religious writing, that makes religion repulsive to so many people. . . . Until now Greene has allowed one to see behind his work only a faith that is an instrument of torture calculated to make any relationship between men and women, and life in the flesh, intolerable.

That is very neat—the only trouble is that it is not true. Mr. West's whole argument falls for the simple reason that Scobie in *The Heart of the Matter* and the priest in *The Power and the Glory* are well on the way to being undone long *before* they reach the "pivotal" point of "contact with female flesh." Further, the torture suffered by both characters was not caused by the faith, but by an *unlived* faith. It was exactly when the priest finally began to live his faith that he was restored to the possibility of finding life tolerable; it was exactly because Scobie failed to *live* his faith that human fellowship became so intolerable that suicide seemed the only way out.

Mr. West is right, I think, about his estimate of *The End of the Affair*, but he is right, unfortunately, for the wrong reasons.

I hope I'm right—and for the right reasons—when, to end, I revise my earlier verdict on the book. It is powerful writing and most rewarding reading and certainly fare for the mature reader —and not only for those professionally interested, as I had over-cautiously cautioned. The language is explicit enough to cause some uneasiness in only two or three sentences, and even those passages rouse such a sense of the real horribleness of the affair that they preclude any titillation.

The weakness of the book lies, I feel, in the introduction of the "miracles," though, granting their presence, they are well handled. I believe that they *do* intrude, for we are not prepared for them by a sufficient portrayal of Sarah's saintly life. Her sacrifice—great as it was, and her conversion—deep as it was, aren't enough to give base to miraculous intervention. Perhaps Greene introduced them to avoid the charge of leaving this story as ambiguous at the end as many thought *The Heart of the Matter* was. At any rate, Mr. West is right when he says this is a more positive book. There is nothing ambiguous about it, either in the values it upholds, the deep and valid sympathy it evokes, or the place it deserves in the world of literature.

This chronological account makes it clear that even the first edition of *Norms for the Novel* was not an entirely new book. In it, I had included much newly utilized older material that seemed to have special bearing on the problem, and I endeavored to bring all the older matter up to date by applying the principles to books recently published. The principles, if indeed they do succeed in reaching that stature, are as valid now as when they were first applied to *A Tree Grows in Brooklyn*; they may seem to have more cogency when they are related, in this second edition, to books published almost twenty years after that stormy petrel.

So much for the first part of *Norms for the Novel*. The second part is a development of articles which, again, appeared first in *America* (September 28, October 5 and 19, 1946). These articles attempted to establish some further principles for judging novels, not from the moral point of view, but on literary grounds. Here we have a book, let us say, which is not immoral (and hence not *ipso facto* ruled out of the realm of literature). Well and good, but there is a further question to be asked about it—what is the intrinsic bent of the book's moral soundness? What does it—or ought it—lead to? How is it oriented? In other and more philosophical words, what is the final cause that informs such a morally good book? (It is to be noted that throughout all this discussion I have steered away from the matter of style, of form. The most morally sound book in the world will not be able to lay claim to being literature if it is not at the same time well written, but that is not my concern in all that follows; I am discussing the content of a book and not the manner of its presentation.)

In order to avoid any misconceptions, may I issue here an important caution to be kept in mind throughout all that follows. It is this: I am not talking about books that are on the Index of Forbidden Books of the Catholic Church. When I say, for example, that "every reader must be his own Index as he reads," I am not advocating the taking of the law into one's own hands. If a book *is* on the Index, and you are a Catholic, you may not read it without permission; if it *is not*, you must still put it aside if it proves to be a temptation to you, even though others may not find it a temptation. Again, when I say that parts do not necessarily condemn the whole, I am not questioning the Church's authority to put a book on the Index precisely because parts of it are dangerous to the general reader. The operative word in the phrase is "necessarily."

PART I
FIVE PRINCIPLES FOR
MORAL EVALUATION

1. The Norm of Objective Charity

A SPIRIT of "fair play" is not, as many consider it for lack of any deeper and wider principles, the highest of Christian virtues—in fact, it may not be a Christian virtue at all, but just a natural offshoot of a spirit of humanitarianism. It can, however, be rooted in the virtue of justice and indeed take on some of the beauty of the virtue of charity. Hence it is that a judgment of a book and assessment of its accord with moral principles, if it is to be done in a Christian spirit, must be done in a spirit of fair play that will be both charitable and just. It is but simple justice both to the author and to the work, and simple charity to them, as well, to give what praise can fairly be attributed while condemning what must be condemned. The review of Sholem Asch's *The Apostle*, printed in full in the Introduction, was written, I hope, in such a spirit. The general terms of the review constitute a rather strong condemnation. But on artistic grounds it was only honest to remark that *The Apostle* was a job far superior to Douglas' *The Robe*. It was superior in characterization, in atmosphere, in that knowledge of the times and customs which is psychological rather than merely factual. This superiority could be and had to be admitted, it would surely seem, without a critic having to anticipate an excoriation for "adroitly boosting" a book he was actually criticizing adversely.

There is, of course, the danger that in trying to be fair and objective to the book itself, the critic may seem to be bending over backward to say kind things about the author. Obviously some of the adverse opinions which occasioned this whole discussion felt that this danger had not been avoided. One of the dissenting opinions, for example, said: "I conclude that Asch

29

is a pompous and evil charlatan. . . . Knowing the trend nowadays of the insidious, practical application of the Asch thesis, I recognize him as a dangerous anti-Christian."

Now, I do not maintain that there can be no judgment of the author by the critic. The author of any piece of literature is *in* his work, and in judging his work I will of necessity have to some extent to judge the author. The point to be made is that I have to *judge him through his work* and *not his work through him*—and particularly *not through his private life*. A man may conceivably be an utter degenerate and still write, let us say, a beautiful nature study. If his moral degeneracy is revealed in the study, the reviewer will be justified in adverting to it. If the study remains pure despite the fouled hands that wrote it, the critic has no right as a critic, and particularly as a Catholic, to castigate the author's private life on the occasion of criticizing a particular book. There may be, of course, the practical advisability at times of adverting to an author's personal immorality so as to caution those who may be led by an admiration of his unobjectionable writing to read others of his works which might be morally dangerous.

What I mean may perhaps best be shown concretely if I quote from my review of Sinclair Lewis' *Kingsblood Royal* (*America*, June 7, 1947):

> But the totally debilitating element against the book's being a piece of literature is the fact that there is no love in it. Mr. Lewis is here quite evidently playing the role of moralist; but a real moralist must be motivated by charity. One cannot escape the impression that Lewis is not really concerned with the injustices suffered by the Negroes, nor really ashamed at the bigotry and hatred of his fellow whites. One wonders whether he would honestly welcome a solution to the "Negro problem"; for if it were or had been solved, he would not have been able to write a sensational book about it.

The same impression has been latent in every Lewis novel—

he is not so much concerned with the reformation of his Elmer Gantry's, his Babbitt's, his Gideon Planish's, as he is with keeping their foibles alive for the incisions of his scalpel, or rather, for the shocks of his bludgeon. . . . Until there shines through his work a sincere and rational affection for people, for human nature, there will be no understanding or sympathy or affection for people to be got from his work by the reader. All we can do in Mr. Lewis' company is to watch an experiment; we never share an experience.

This, I must admit, is a judgment on Sinclair Lewis. But it is a critical judgment validated, I think, by what is objectively present (or plainly absent) in his books; it is not a judgment of his own subjective morality. Maybe Mr. Lewis was brimming over with love for his fellow man; maybe he was (I sincerely pray so) plunged deep in love of God. All I can say is: I don't see it in his books.

Again, in reviewing the notorious *From Here to Eternity*, James Jones' angry and sensational war book of early 1951, I remarked (*America*, March 10, 1951), while thoroughly condemning the book:

Let me say unhesitatingly that I recognize, with many of the critics, that Mr. Jones can write—not flawlessly, but tempestuously, passionately, if almost maudlinly at times. I can even respect what is being called his "honesty." He has something to say and feels that he *must* say it. He has a love for the rough, brutalized companionship of the Army as he apparently knew it, and a hatred for the "system" (as he also apparently knew it), and both clamor for voice. He has given them voice, all right—a raucous, obscene voice. This may be the only voice Mr. Jones possesses or recognizes, and so, perhaps he himself is not too much to be censured.

This, again, may be a judgment on Mr. Jones, but it is a judgment arrived at through the book, and not one based upon Mr. Jones' private life.

The preceding brief discussion on "fair play" brings to the fore a principle which I believe is cardinal both in literary criticism and in reading—*what is to be judged is the book and not the author*. I, too, may perhaps recognize that *The Apostle* is "anti-Christian." I certainly recognize that Mr. Asch's subsequent book, *Moses*, distorted to an extent two of the master ideas of early biblical history, the ideas of the priesthood and of sacrifice. But from this evidence I cannot say that I know Asch is a "charlatan." All I can say is that Asch is wrong, but for all I know he may be a saint; his book is wrong, but I must, until my presumption may have to yield to proof of the contrary, give him credit for being sincere in writing it.

This imputation of motives is an easy fault for Catholic readers and critics to fall into, particularly if the author is treating subjects that touch upon religious truths we hold precious. We revere so deeply the Mass, the sacraments, the person of Our Lord and our Lady, that we find it hard to conceive how someone can be at variance with our devotion and still be sincere. There was, for example, a venerable and learned priest I knew who simply could not be persuaded to read Werfel's *The Song of Bernadette*, because he felt that there was some sort of contradiction or indignity in a Jew's writing about our Lady. The obvious question put to him, of course, was "and what was our Lady?"

But an honest critic cannot yield to such one-sided judgments, particularly if he happens to be at the same time a critic and a Catholic. A book must be judged on its own merits, first and always on its literary merits, on its doctrinal, historical and philosophical merits when the subject matter warrants it. Asch's *The Apostle* and, to a lesser extent, *Moses*, ranked fairly high in literary qualities but were misleading in their doctrinal and historical aspects. Such books as *The Robe* and Douglas' last novel, *The Big Fisherman*, were equally misleading in doctrine and history and decidedly less competent in literary artistry. If that judgment is correct, which of the two authors has been more thoroughly—and I hope in a spirit of fairness—criticized, particularly for Catholic readers?

One aspect of the modern novel that has proved a fertile field for imputation of unworthy motives to the author is the depiction of priest and nun characters. Here again the reaction of many Catholic readers is motivated by their respect for the clergy and religious, but it is at times a respect that leads to an overzealous and intemperate—and needless—defense. The fact that several priests in *The Keys of the Kingdom* and two of them in *The Power and the Glory* were either not too perfect or even downright bad, need not by any means prove that Cronin or Greene was bent on traducing the clergy. Many readers are all too ready to think that because one such character is painted, the diabolically inspired author is saying that *all* priests and nuns are of like stripe.

This is not so, and, as a matter of fact, the better the craftsmanship of an author, the less probability will there be that his delineation of individual characters will water them down into mere types. The little "whisky priest" in *The Power and the Glory* is a sharply etched individual, he is like no one else, and it is therefore impossible for any intelligent reader, I believe, to see him as representative of a class. Great—and even merely good—writers always give us individuals; if characters in a book are merely typical, the book is necessarily second rate. Pickwick is Pickwick and no one else, and it would be foolish to think that Dickens was trying to say, through Pickwick, that all Englishmen are jolly, romantic and impractical.

It is possible, of course, that over a period of time and through many books an author may build up an impression that does argue a tendency to make sweeping generalizations. James T. Farrell does give the unmistakable impression that he feels that most—if not all—of the Irish who live or lived in slum areas are doomed to frustration and more or less degeneracy. But this is a judgment that Mr. Farrell has forced on his readers as a sort of cumulative reaction. And if an author were to conjure up in book after book morally bad priest or nun characters, we would certainly be justified in thinking that he was at least obsessed with the thought, if not positively determined to misrepresent.

Taking all these variations and possibilities into consideration, the general principle is still valid: it is the book that is subject to judgment and not the author, save insofar as he reveals himself in the book or in the totality of his writing. Even when he does so reveal himself, the Christian judgment of him will be, if it must be, that he is wrong or misinformed or shortsighted—and not immediately that he is insincere or a charlatan. That judgment may indeed finally have to be passed, but it ought to be the final judgment and not the first.

This principle of objective charity in criticism was given striking emphasis by the late Pope Pius XII in a unique allocution. I commented on this address in the April 14, 1956, issue of *America*; my remarks are reprinted in full here:

The late H. L. Mencken once wrote of himself: "The plain fact is that I am not a fair man and don't want to hear both sides. On all subjects, from aviation to xylophone, I have fixed and invariable ideas." This may be read, of course, as a frankly disarming confession which leaves no room for discussion. Unfortunately, however, this attitude of mind was regarded, particularly when Mencken was the Samuel Johnson of Baltimore, but even later when appreciative obituaries were being written, as a sort of irrefutable proof that he was a great critic of the American scene precisely because he always, so to speak, came out swinging.

An allocution of the late Pope Pius XII contains this maxim: "A critic habitually ruled by passion ought never even take his pen in hand." The reason for this, the Holy Father had indicated in the immediate context, is that the critic, in addition to having intellectual competence, must always be on his guard lest the bent of his will and his personal sensitivities set him *a priori* at odds with the object of his criticism. On the contrary, it is imperative that the critic observe, as far as he can, a strict objectivity, and "open his soul to sentiments of good will and confidence in the author he is criticizing, unless certain, positive and grave reasons" make this openness of soul impossible.

It would be difficult, I think, to find two statements on the role of criticism more at odds—though it must be admitted in all honesty that Mr. Mencken was constructing no theory of criticism. He was simply telling us how he worked, nor was he saying he was not fair toward the work of any individual author. Nevertheless, he was professing, even boasting, of an unobjective mind and would be, I think, the type of critic the Holy Father had in view. This bias in Mencken will go far, I feel, to assure that his critical studies (of movements rather than of specific authors) will soon echo, if at all, like rumors of far-off, unmeaning strawman battles.

The Pope's statement occurred in an allocution that is, as far as I can determine, unique in the history of the Papacy. On February 13, 1956, Pius XII received in audience a group organized by the editors of *Letture*, a literary review edited by the Italian Jesuits in Milan. He chose as the topic of his discourse "The Duties of Catholic Criticism," by which he meant Catholic literary criticism. This is the first time a Supreme Pontiff has expatiated at such length and so explicitly on that subject.

This brief summary of the Pope's remarks has been taken from a comparison of the text in the *Osservatore Romano* (February 13–14) with that which appeared in *La Documentation Catholique* (March 4). This portion of his remarks, the Pope tells us, will deal only with the "subject" of criticism, by which he means the critic and his qualifications. At another time, "when the occasion presents itself," he will speak of the "object," which I take to mean the work on which the critic exercised himself.

All who are engaged in the work of criticism, whether in the classroom or in the pages of the Catholic press, will take heart and bend to their work with deeper devotion because of what His Holiness says about the apostolate of criticism. He recognizes in all who work in this field "strong and faithful cooperators" in his pastoral ministry. He does not "need to emphasize how great is the necessity, nobility and importance" of sane and competent criticism, especially in these days, when reading matter has "considerable influence over the fate of individuals and the community." Moreover, "criticism exercised according to the norms of truth and of ethics" may appeal particularly to the modern man, who likes to "form his own judgments," but who nevertheless will accept the suggestions of criticism that has succeeded in "inspiring confidence."

Nor does the Pope intend, as he explicitly states, to restrict the role of the Catholic critic to passing judgments on the moral aspects of the work under scrutiny. Scientific, literary and artistic aspects must also come under the purview of the Catholic critic. In this way, criticism will win respect in the public mind, and will be totally in accord with the perennial tradition of the Church, which always leaves the cultures of the world by following the development of thought and art.

One forceful passage, which I wish could be called to the attention of every critic in the world, and especially to those working in this country, runs:

> The heights and depths to which literature rises or falls depend in notable part on the critics, according to the degree of the perspicacity, honesty and force of mind they prove they possess. . . . [For] if a reader recurs to criticism, it is because he believes in the critic's knowledge, honesty and maturity.

The Pope is realist enough to put down as the first requirement —though he does it with a rather smiling apology for even mentioning it—that the critic read the book. But what kind of reading? "Simple intellectual knowledge is not enough, because the critic is something more than a mere reporter." He must also pass judgment, from a "dispassionate consideration of the pros and cons," from which alone can come the critic's "yes" or "no" in each individual case. Only after such a reading can "criticism receive its definite form and be presented for publication."

It is at this point that Pius XII remarks on the positive need for objectivity mentioned above. However, he again is a realist. He notes that though "nobility of character and goodness of heart are always the best armor in any contest," nevertheless, "in criticism ideas and opinions are often at odds." Nor are nobility and goodness to be taken as synonymous with naïveté and credulity. Objectivity, in fact, cannot function if there is any lack in probity, firmness and incorruptibility of character, defects that might lead the critic to be so "noble" and "good" as to write to please author, publisher or public.

Firmness of character in the critic, we are told, will be shown in his publishing, calmly and without fear, his considered and objective judgment, and in defending that judgment if it is attacked. Just as a judge who would not have the courage to defend the laws ought to be unseated, so should the critic abandon his work if he loves a quiet life more than the truth.

Having established these general qualities necessary in the critic, the Holy Father then goes on to enumerate three maxims that ought to guide the critic in a practical manner. The first is a dictum of Tacitus, in which the Roman historian states that it is the duty of the historian to write *sine ira et studio* (without passion or partiality). Expanding this thought, the Pope explains that it does not mean that a critic must deal in luke-warm, wishy-washy style or thought. A calm and moderate criticism has the perfect right, for example, to speak out with strong and vigorous indignation against pornographic literature. Nor can the critic be accused of partiality who takes as the rule of his judgment Christian truth in its purity and integrity. Righteous indignation against evil and evident adherence to Christian truth are not passion and partiality.

The second practical rule for the critic's guidance is: *verbum oris est verbum mentis* (may we translate, "a man writes or speaks as he thinks"?). Accordingly, says the Pontiff, "if one wants to know the mind of the author, one listens to his words, and as long as there are no positive reasons to call them into doubt, one will consider the author's words as the natural witness to his inner thoughts."

This seems simple and obvious, but the applications are rich. From this it follows that what the critic judges is not the author but his work: ". . . the person of the author, his life and his tendencies ought not be the starting point for critical investigation, but the work and what is expressed in it." If the maxim calls upon the author to be sincere, to speak precisely as he thinks, it is no less a challenge to the critic to interpret favorably all that is objectively susceptible of favorable interpretation. But again, this presumption in favor of the sense the author intends in no way prevents the critic from pointing out errors if they exist. This habitual inclination toward favorable interpretation of another's words or actions, the Pope states in a wise aside, is a necessity for peaceful coexistence among men in their reciprocal relationships.

The Pope's final practical norm is *super omnia caritas* (above all, charity). The critic must address himself to the work in a spirit of charity. But what will be the rule when there seems to be a conflict between charity and truth? It may happen that the critic feels that if he speaks the truth as he sees it, he will offend and even injure the author. Which will take precedence? The critic will remember that he has a duty of truth not only with regard to the author, but also with regard to the reader. He will therefore safeguard both charity and truth by preventing dangerous misunderstandings on the part of the reader, while at the same time remaining courteous toward the author. "The foundation is truth; the crown is charity." These principles

. . . ought to hold first place in the delicate work of literary criticism. . . . They are the principal means by which to merit the confidence the public will place in criticism, and they mark off for the critic the bounds of justice and injustice in the accomplishment of his important function.

Pope Pius XII did not live to issue the second part of his suggestions to critics, but this priceless document without doubt underscores the point I have been striving to make in this first chapter: the absolutely basic norm, for both the critic in his approach to the work, and for the reader in his appreciation of the work *and* the criticism of it, is the norm of objective charity.

(*The full text of the Pope's address may be found in the* Catholic Mind, *September, 1956, pp. 530–36.*)

2. Objectional Parts and Total Effect

A SECOND principle of moral judgment was brought to the fore by several stormy letters and accusatory reviews which took *America* to task for its "recommendation" of the then famous *A Tree Grows in Brooklyn*. Unfortunately, this type of accusation has by no means ceased. It can continue to be anticipated on the occasion of the publication of any novel that is hailed as "realistic." It continues to recur in varied forms on the occasion of reviews of such books as Graham Greene's *The Heart of the Matter* and *The End of the Affair*, Herman Wouk's *The Caine Mutiny* and *Marjorie Morningstar*, and Henry Morton Robinson's *The Cardinal*. Its latest recrudescence occurred on the publication of Kathryn Hulme's *The Nun's Story* and of Morris L. West's *The Devil's Advocate*.

This type of accusation is based explicitly or implicitly on a philosophical principle which is certainly sound in itself but often misapplied in literary criticism. The principle reads, *bonum ex integra causa, malum ex quocumque defectu.* This is a little difficult to translate with concise accuracy, but perhaps we may use the phrase "good demands fullness of being; evil results from any defect." If the axiom is translated in oversimple style to read "a thing is good when there is not a flaw in it, but a single flaw makes it evil" (a translation that has been applied to this aspect of literature we are discussing), it shoots far wide of the mark. If such a version were applied, for example, as the criterion of a good man, it would force us to say that a single moral defect, no matter how slight, makes him an evil man. This obviously is nonsense. And even when applied to the artistic sphere, such an oversimple translation would still make no sense. A flaw in a painting or a statue does not necessarily make it a bad work of art; it prevents it from being perfect, but it may still be excellent.

What the axiom really means, of course, is that if anything —a human act, a material object, and so on—is marred by the least defect, the least lack of the perfection that is connatural to it, it cannot be called *simpliciter bonum* (totally good); but the presence of such a defect by no means renders the thing *simpliciter malum* (totally bad). Perhaps a workable paraphrase of the philosophical axiom would read, "We call a thing good for its function when all the essential qualities required for the work are present in reasonable fullness." The operative words in such a definition are "essential" and "reasonable."

The same line of reasoning should govern judgment passed upon books. We need not necessarily come to the conclusion that a book which is predominantly moral in tone becomes a morally bad book because of a single suggestive passage or even a number of such passages.

The effect of these passages has to be judged against the background of the whole moral import of the work. Such passages, it seems, would be analogous to the circumstances of the moral act which, together with the intrinsic finality of the act and its motivation, constitute the ultimate norm of morality of human acts.

So much, then, for the principle. How does it work out when applied to such books as *A Tree Grows in Brooklyn* and *The End of the Affair*, to Morris West's *The Devil's Advocate* and John Buell's *The Pyx?* Let us grant, merely for the sake of the argument and without conceding it, that there are suggestive passages in these books. Must the books be therefore sweepingly condemned as having been written "with a total disregard of decency"? To hold this is surely to have missed the meaning and message of the novels. The whole burden of the first novel rests on the thesis that character can dominate environment.

It is precisely the fundamental decency of Francie, the little girl growing up in the near-slums, and the decency of her hard-working mother and even of her genially besotted father, which envelops the book in an atmosphere of the Christian virtue of hope. The whole family hopes and works upon the hope that they can keep uncontaminated by their environment; the author hopes for and with them and, by implication, for others also born into such a world.

Similarly, in *The End of the Affair* Mr. Greene is saying over and over again through the diary of Sarah, the adulterous wife, that the time may well come when even the undeniable attractions of a purely sensual love will prove utterly inadequate to fill the void left by the absence of God's love.

West's strong tale hints at homosexuality, for instance, but its theme is the reality of sanctity and the Church's realism in knowing that sanctity can bud from the most apparently hostile environment. Similarly, *The Pyx*, with its subject matter of very literal diabolism, is focused ultimately on faith and reverence.

These themes are sound and of deep importance. This is the first impression that the books will make upon the reader who is not unduly sensitive. If, in making their point, the authors introduce one or other passages which might possibly have been toned down to some extent, it is certainly but the exercise of a balanced judgment to weigh the impact of these passages (perhaps not too happy) against the impact of the total work (without doubt on the side of the angels). This is by no means to say that the message, the atmosphere, the total force of the book, is a completely justifying reason for dragging in possibly suggestive passages. But it *is* to say that to miss the whole story, the effective force behind the book and the operative virtue in the book, and to concentrate exclusively on the shocking passages, is but poorly to exercise the function of critic or balanced reader.

42

But was *A Tree Grows in Brooklyn*, to take this as an example, dotted with unduly sensational passages? Can we grant that? I held when I reviewed the book, and still hold, that there is not one obscene passage in all of the 443 pages. Even the rather melodramatic scene when Francie is unsuccessfully attacked by the pervert is objectively told; there is no allure to it, no incitement, and it fits quite normally into the development of the story and of the girl's character. Through it, she comes to realize more deeply her mother's deep and even fierce protective love.

The language of the book *is* vulgar, but what other language could the author employ? Could she say, "You see, Francie heard some awful, but positively awful, words as she was growing up, and I think you know the ones I mean"? How real would that have been? How honest? To picture a child growing up in the slums, the slums have to be pictured as they are, and they are, we understand, not lovely.

This problem of the frequency of vulgar language (not obscenity, mark) is a test of artistic discipline, I admit. It is the true craftsman who can suggest that a character uses such language constantly, without actually placing it in his mouth in every sentence. But we are not here discussing the desiderata of artistic skill; we are asking simply whether plain vulgar language, the famous four-letter words, are enough, of themselves, to condemn a book as being obscene. And whether a reader be disgusted and repelled by such language is, again, another point. The critic can but warn him.

Indeed, even in the matter of apparent blasphemy in a book, the answer is not simply to say that the presence of such phrases *ipso facto* condemns the book. Father Louis A. Rongione of the Department of Philosophy at Villanova University, quoted in *The Catholic Library World* (April, 1951, p. 210) makes this sane observation: "The mere presence of blasphemy in a book is not sufficient to condemn a book unless the author gives indication of condoning it or presenting it in a light and offensive way. Again, one must be careful, whether or not there is a real case of formal blasphemy, which requires two conditions: a) use of language which reviles God or His actions, or arrogates to creatures prerogatives of the Creator; b) advertence to the fact that such language dishonors God. Undoubtedly many of the characters in a book who are portrayed as using such language are of a type not to know that they are materially blaspheming."

To advert to my second practical example, I do not believe that the passages thought objectionable in *The End of the Affair* can be justly called pornographic. They come as an undoubted shock to some readers. But I believe that the mature reader will find in them no titillation, no inducement to morbid reliving of the scenes, no temptation. It is precisely because they *do* come as such a shock that they carry with them a sense almost of revulsion, just as the experience itself ultimately aroused in Sarah the same feeling.

From what has been said can we venture to indicate the legitimate audience for such books as *A Tree Grows in Brooklyn*, *The End of the Affair*, *The Devil's Advocate*, *The Pyx* and many a forthcoming book which will pose the same problem? Can such books be recommended by a Catholic reviewer? I hold yes—when and if the reviewer, remembering that he is not merely judging a piece of literature but also addressing himself to a large undefinable mass of readers, makes the necessary prudential remarks. If you are warned, for example, that a book contains much vulgar talk and you simply do not like vulgar passages, then you have been given a sufficient guide in the matter. If you can take vulgar passages in stride without being irked or unduly impressed, and feel that the review indicates that deeper qualities to be found in the book will more than make up for the passages, then you have been given sound guidance toward the gold that far outvalues the dross.

The same observation is to be made as well on books that go beyond vulgarity into more or less explicit description in sensual matters. Apart from books which are clearly and unabashedly obscene—and fortunately not many appear on the American scene in any given year—there *is* a question of degree. The Canon Law of the Catholic Church itself allows for this in the provisions laid down concerning the classes of prohibited literature. According to the common interpretation, a book falls under the category of obscene literature if the obscenity is explicit, if it can reasonably be judged to be a direct intention of the author and if it is prominent. Prominence would be judged to exist if a large section of the text—a whole chapter, for example—presented obscenity thus explicitly and directly. (I refer the reader here to Rev. Redmond A. Burke, C.S.V., *What Is the Index?* Bruce, 1952.)

Apart from these canonical provisions, personal reactions enter into each one's own evaluation. Some who are more sensitive or delicate or fastidious or perhaps just plain scrupulous might be disturbed, for example, by the very mention of the word "adultery." Others honestly experience no trouble even in passages which are somewhat detailed. Here again such a book can be recommended if the reviewer speaks in prudential fashion, as he may very well do under such inclusive phrases as "the discriminate," "the mature," "the adult," "the poised," reader. A possible hitch here, of course, is that any curious person who wants to read this type of book can very easily say to himself, "Oh, but *I'm* the discriminating reader." The only reply to this is simply that one must be sincere with oneself and not hurl objections at the critic's remarks because one has rushed in where prior experience may have showed him he dare not tread.

It must be kept in mind that this whole discussion thus far has nothing to do with convincing people that their taste should be changed. This type of book—somewhat vulgar, somewhat suggestive—may not appeal to you at all: well and good. You may not like Beethoven, Brahms or Bach as much as you like Count Basie or the latest ruler in the realm of rock 'n' roll. It would be possible, I believe, for one who knows music well to convince you that there are more reasons for liking the three Bs better than Count B. But that is another point. We are concerned here simply with the question of grounds for issuing blanket condemnations, and I am firmly convinced that not a few Catholics, readers and critics, do considerable harm to the reputation of Catholic intelligence by forgetting that any normal, balanced reader can be solidly enough grounded in faith and morals and taste not to find some vulgar expressions or some frankly descriptive passages sources of "mental and moral infection."

If that is not true, then Catholic education is raising hothouse plants indeed. Not that we ought to have courses in vulgarity as a part of our curriculum so that Catholics will recognize it when they meet it. But our courses in both literature and religion ought to equip future readers with mental stability and moral poise enough to read books that are "realistic." There, the horrid word is out. But let it just stay here for a while, since a further section in this treatise will deal at length with "realism."

Let us go on to a more general statement on this whole rather complex subject. Perhaps it is possible to lay down some general workable principles about what does or does not constitute a morally objectionable book. An openly obscene book is objectionable; of that there is no doubt. But what of a book that must not be so stigmatized? May it be read by some? How can we tell?

Admittedly it is quite difficult to say a final and definitive word on the question of morality or its contrary in literature. This is not because moral principles are themselves vague and shifting; they are eternal and immutable; but the neatness with which they can be applied to a specific book shifts and changes in almost kaleidoscopic variety, as the moral climate of human acts filters through to us in the author's presentation.

There are, however, two cardinal principles by which we can test the moral soundness and decency of a work of literature. Let us confine "literature" here to the field of fiction because it is precisely here that the problem most frequently arises. These two principles are, I feel, about the only "rules of the game" we have. And even one of them, as we shall see, is so much subject to personal application that it really does not measure up with complete satisfaction to the stature of a general, all-inclusive, immutable norm.

3. Recognition of Sin for What It Is

THE FIRST of these two cardinal principles hinted at in the preceding chapter's conclusion may be stated this way: if sin is discussed or portrayed in a story, it must be recognized for what it is. Theologically this is sound, for perhaps the greatest of all sins is the philosophizing or the laughing of sin out of existence. Here precisely lies the insidious danger of those books and movies which proclaim to unthinking millions in tones of varying seductiveness: "Marital infidelity? Oh no. This is not infidelity, this is romance. Don't you see that they were made for one another?" Or: "Unscrupulous and ruthless exercise of power? Oh no, this is a clever bit of business strategy"—for don't think that it is only the Sixth Commandment which is shrugged out of existence by modern amoralists.

From the purely literary viewpoint, as well, the reality behind this axiom is implicit in the very nature of literature. For not only drama, but the whole range of literature draws to some extent its sustenance and vigor from the element of conflict. This is not surprising if you but recall that life, which literature is supposed to mirror and interpret, is itself "a warfare upon earth." This truth can be illustrated and confirmed in almost all areas of literary work. In some, the conflict is, as it were, external to the theme of the work. In others, it enters into the very fiber of the story or action. The short lyric or nature piece hints at conflict, at struggle, if only at the struggle in the author's efforts to reduce the world's or the soul's beauty to the discipline and form of verse or sensitive prose. The lower ranges of comedy have as their necessary theme clashes of temperament and will which are happily resolved. Tragedy *is* the story of conflict. And the novel, too, depends largely (style, of course, is an absolute essential, but that is not the point under consideration) for its substance and permanence on the degree to which the element of conflict is present in the story's and the characters' development. Even under the apparently placid surface of Marquand's novels, for example, there is a whole world of comico-tragic tension and stress.

Now if this be true, namely that conflict is always the felt and implicit atmosphere, if not always the explicit theme, of all literature (and the more obviously so as literature becomes more deeply concerned with the analysis and interpretation of human values), then it follows that sin must be recognized for what it is. For if it is not so recognized, then there is no reason why good ought to be acknowledged as good or evil as evil, and if there is no difference between good and evil, if all values shade off into a dull and neutral gray, then there is no conflict possible, save on the subhuman level of sheer instinct and feeling, much like the conflict of two dogs snarling over a bone.

The principle, then, is true and, I believe, rather obvious. But its application must be cautious and temperate. Some questions arise immediately, and the reader must have been waiting to get a word in edgewise to ask them. *By whom*, he asks, must sin be recognized as sin? By the author? By the characters who are portrayed as sinning? By the reader? By all readers? Here two matters have perhaps got intertwined, and it will be a good preliminary step to untangle them. One is the question of the greatness of the author and his book; the other is the fitness of the book for general reading.

If the author recognizes sin completely and adequately for what it is, his book (granting his eminence in other elements of his craft) will be a great book. For sin is an offense against God, a loss of His friendship, and surely that theme (and of course its obverse, repentance and restoration) is of all the most sublime. Let the author, well equipped with the other tools of his trade, grasp and vitalize that theme and we will have another *Divine Comedy,* another *Confessions* of St. Augustine. This is precisely what makes for the greatness that is certainly present in the theme (how well it is handled is a further question) of *Brideshead Revisited, The Power and the Glory, The Heart of the Matter, The End of the Affair.* Waugh and Greene —and we might mention, of course, Mauriac and the French Catholic authors, some of the Irish and a few Americans—show through their characters that they have grasped to a quite profound extent this primary aspect of sin—namely, that it is a loss of the greatest possible good.

But we have no right to demand such depth of appreciation from any one author all the time or from all authors at any one time. Indeed, no one, even the person in whom a realization of sin's malice is strong, can ever fully comprehend that malice. The closer an author approaches this realization, the greater his work will be, but his realization may not be so adequate and yet his whole work may be good and eminently worth reading. Sigrid Undset's realization of this fundamental disorder of sin is far deeper, for example, than John P. Marquand's. For Marquand sin is sin, not exactly for the reason that it loses God's friendship, but rather because it sets the individual off center, confuses his aims and makes life pointless. This, of course, is true, and if an author does no more than approach the problem in this way, he may indeed be missing the heights —or the depths—but he is safe from the charge that he has completely glossed sin over.

Here we touch on what seems to me the prime objection to the claim of such a writer as Hemingway to be a truly great novelist. He has many of the gifts of a great novelist. He is, in addition, as almost every critic has pointed out, a crusader. He is always for the underdog. He, too, would want fair play in the world—but he wants it for no ultimate moral reason that I have ever been able to discover. As Wyndham Lewis put it in the Summer, 1934, issue of the now defunct *American Review*, "[He and all his characters] are in the multitudinous ranks of *those to whom things happen.*" His characters do not will, they make no choice; the same unreasoned reasons that impelled Jordan (in *For Whom the Bell Tolls*) to fight for the Spanish Loyalists might just as well have hustled him over into the camp of "the Fascists."

This curious lack of a moral fiber in Hemingway's characters, resulting from the absence of true conflict, was pointed out by Michael F. Moloney in his study of Hemingway in *Fifty Years of the American Novel* (Scribner, 1951, p. 196). His final judgment is: "Hemingway's naturalism is always promising to break through its isolation and to link up with the world of spirit. But the promise is never quite achieved. It is this failure which will go heaviest against him in the final summing up. . . . The obliqueness of his characters derives from his refusal or inability (whether he is the unconscious or willing captive of his age is a nice question) to give evidence to that potential in man which either raises him above or sinks him below the rest of the animal world." This judgment is confirmed, it seems to me, by Hemingway's latest, *The Old Man and the Sea*, despite the wide critical acclaim it has received. This short novel, by the way, is a fine example of naturalistic technique at its best. It exemplifies the fact that naturalism need not always lead an author into the quicksands of pornography; it also betrays a "philosophy" which at base is nothing more than canonization of mere physical courage as the Stoic ideal that can snatch inner victory from apparent outer defeat. This I still maintain, though many a critic read into *The Old Man and the Sea* a Christian symbolism that seems to me farfetched. We shall have to wait for more of the "reformed" Hemingway be-

51

fore we can equate him with an Undset in this matter of "sin" and its recognition.

Incidentally, the short novel (the "novella"), of which *The Old Man and the Sea* is a superb technical example, is one of the finest fields for study in this matter of conflict. By its very compression it sets in high relief the forces that are often present, but somewhat dissipated in longer works. The spiritual aspects of the conflict, muted in Hemingway, are superbly present in Paul Horgan's short novels. Three of them, *The Devil in the Desert, One Red Rose for Christmas* and *To the Castle*, are published in *Humble Powers*.

A still more glaring example of how this moral dilution quite neatly emasculates an author's work is to be found in much of Sinclair Lewis. It is, indeed, more evident in him because his writing has not the stylistic tensity and the air of conviction that cloak Hemingway's fundamental weakness. It may perhaps be summed up by saying that Lewis is not a good hater; he is very much and very shrilly annoyed at a lot of people and things, but the basis for conflict is destroyed because it is not good and evil that clash in his stories, but complacency and irritation.

The author, then, must recognize sin as sin, at least in the minimum sense of seeing it as a source of disturbance, or imbalance, in human relationships. Here a delicate point arises. In a criticism (by Father John Ford, S.J., in *Theological Studies*, December, 1944, p. 502) of the first edition of *Tenets for Readers and Reviewers*, Father Ford remarks that such a minimum recognition of sin "does not seem to demand that the author recognize evil, which alone after all, is sin as such. The fact is that many writers do not recognize it or write as though they did not. The result is that their work is permeated with a non-Christian, implicitly anti-Christian atmosphere and philosophy." This comment is, of course, eminently true, and I shall have something to say about such writing further on when the problems of realism and naturalism come up.

Here the question, however, is: may an author legitimately prescind from the moral effects of sin and concentrate on merely what may be called the sociological effects? May he portray, let us say, the social ravages caused by drunkenness without passing judgment on the actual sinfulness of the character's action?—an approach that was used quite successfully in Charles Jackson's *The Lost Weekend*. I believe the answer must be yes, as long as the author does not suggest that there *is* no moral wrong. Admittedly it is quite hard at times to determine neatly whether an author is merely prescinding from the intrinsic morality of his characters' actions or covertly suggesting that these actions are no more than mere social aberrations. Sinclair Lewis, I feel, gives the impression, to take but one of his books, that he really did not think there was anything morally wrong with the marital irregularities that spattered the pages of *Cass Timberlane*. *From Here to Eternity* is another book of this destructive nature; Steinbeck, at least up to the publication of *East of Eden*, seemed to espouse the same view, and so did James Gould Cozzens in *By Love Possessed*. John Marquand, on the other hand, gives the impression in typical works like *So Little Time* and *Point of No Return*, and up to his latest, *Sincerely, Willis Wayde* and *Women and Thomas Harrow*, that if he were queried on this point he would say: "Yes, I realize fully that marital infidelity is wrong before God. What I want to stress, however, is that it is social folly as well." To call it social folly is not, by any means, to tell the whole truth. But neither is it necessarily to *deny* further truth.

To go a step further, must the characters themselves be portrayed as knowing fully that their sin is sin, in the sense of being a moral evil and an offense of God? Not necessarily or always, though the common run of human nature is such and must be such that men actually do know when they are doing right or wrong. But not infrequently the precise verisimilitude

53

of a character portrayed will stem from the fact that a soul can be so disturbed or confused or has so blunted its sensibilities that little moral sense here and now exists or operates. This, I believe, is what gives the peculiar poignancy to the character of Scobie in Graham Greene's *The Heart of the Matter*. He does, indeed, realize with the profoundest conviction that sin—his sin—has been an affront to God's friendship; he feels that his sins have already damned him. But ultimately, when he takes the fatal draught, the struggle between this conviction and the simultaneous realization that God's love is still drawing him had so plunged him into confusion that there seemed to be only one way out. In one sense, Scobie's moral sensibility grows keener as the action progresses; in another sense, it gets duller.

Even so, and for the literary reason we have been pondering, the sense that *something* is wrong about sin must be kept as the bare minimum in the characters' reactions, else the whole basis for conflict goes by the board. It is when a character slides from one moral lapse into another without the least suspicion of evil in his actions or their consequences and without the slightest twinge of uneasiness, regret or remorse, that we have to condemn the book as false in its portrayal of nature. As Geoffrey Stone has written (*American Review*, April, 1937) in discussing "Morals and Poetry":

> Since this choice [of the will between good and evil] is man's most "human" activity, to exclude it from the realm of poetry is to make of poetry, no matter what beauties will find reflection in it, no more than the music of an Aeolian harp; freed from the responsibilities of choice, it is so free that it is no longer art, if by art one understands what is contrived and made. . . . When a false philosophy is developed to a point where it cuts the poet off from the common moral territory entirely, it vitiates almost everything he writes.

In this connection I would like to call attention to a small but very stimulating book by Nathan Comfort Starr, *The Dynamics of Literature* (Columbia University Press, 1945). In the chapter on "The True and Lively Word" (p. 20), Dr. Starr has this pertinent remark about the point here under discussion:

> By its very medium of expression, writing . . . is strongly social by nature. Its field is not so much knowledge as conduct. For no matter whether the central character reflects or acts, whether he stands isolated or plays his part in a large group of society, the author's concern is always the problem of human satisfaction. Wordsworth rightly called the poet a man speaking to men. Very often this sense of the kinship between the poet and his fellow man is revealed in terms of definite ethical responsibility. This is especially true of English literature, in which from the earliest days the reflective and even introspective Anglo-Saxon mind has shown a strong moral bent. Whether or not such conscious judgments are part of the work, it is impossible to conceive of literature divorced from the problem of our endless search for the good in human experience.

I shall have occasion later to refer to this thoughtful and good little book.

"The common moral territory"—that is the essential point. And it may be said that relatively few novels published today by respectable American firms fall completely outside that norm. There are plenty of "speckled books." There are many each year against which some cautions have to be issued for reasons of prudence, but there are by no means—a fact for which we can be grateful—legions of books that deserve the charge that they are entirely rotten. Indeed, such books could not very well be published in large numbers, for the vast mass even of immature readers is simply not interested in characters who are so atrophied they are just not human beings. One may be, indeed, interested in glancing at their gyrations as robots; one cannot be concerned in investigating their fate as humans.

This sense of sin, accordingly, at the very least in the realization that it is a wrong and a source of conflict, if not in the higher sense that it is a loss of God's friendship, must in some way color a portrayal or a discussion of sin in literature.

A most important point here arises for the intelligent reading of literature which deals with the subject of sin. It is this: sin need not necessarily be portrayed as punished in a specific story. The novel may be a good novel, though it ends with the wrongdoer prosperous and respected and even speciously happy. Catholic readers are too often shortsightedly demanding on this point. They feel that if the author does not, as it were, crack down on the sinner in his book he is automatically condoning the wrongdoing.

This is false, first, from a literary point of view, because if the inevitability of the punishment has not been built up legitimately in the plot and in the development of character, any unmotivated introduction of punishment will be a *deus ex machina*. More than that, insistence that punishment must always be meted out in the story betrays a mentality that is basically materialistic, because it conceives that this world is, after all, the neatly bounded and all-encompassing arena of human actions. The whole story of a life, in this view, must be packed within the confines of earthly existence. This, of course, runs totally counter to the Christian concept that life is not completed here on earth. A character in a book, therefore, may come to the end of his life with the moral balance still askew. That is, indeed, as far as the author, without indulging in fantasy, can take his character. He cannot penetrate into eternity and portray the final punishment of that character's wrongdoing. This was the ultimate question that many readers felt was compromisingly left unanswered at the end of Greene's *The Heart of the Matter*. Why didn't Greene *say* whether Scobie went to heaven or to hell? Greene's justified artistic answer would be: "I don't know or care."

This, however, leads us directly into a further question, the question of how far sin can legitimately be made attractive in a novel. It perhaps ought to be noted here, by way of parenthesis and as a theological basis for what is to follow, that sin *is* attractive. If it were not, no sin would ever be committed, for, as the moralists tell us, sin is never committed *because* it is sinful, but because it always elicits our consent *sub specie boni* (under the appearance of good). But how far that attractiveness may be made vivid in the pages of a book is something else again. It *has* to be made vivid enough to portray the characters as being sufficiently swayed to yield to it. But it *cannot* be made so attractive that the reader, in his turn, is so swayed by the attractiveness as to have his judgment warped and his conduct misdirected. Despite what will be said later about the "sympathy" (or the "empathy," in more recent critical terminology) that good literature ought to foster between reader and character, the reader can never legitimately identify himself fully with a character. Those who think they are Napoleon are, after all, put away safely.

This is a psychological problem, and many tomes have been written about it. How is one to feel the necessary spirit of kinship, of sympathy and understanding with the characters of a novel, and yet preserve one's own independence, which will forestall any identification of one's ideals with the perhaps lamentable ideals of some character? Authors have resorted to the phrase "esthetic distance," or "psychical distance," to describe the necessary detachment which enters into the contemplation of any artifact. If it is true that the viewer of a still life, let us say, of a table spread with succulent viands should not experience the reaction of having his mouth water, it is equally true that one who reads of sin that proved fatally attractive to a character ought not feel himself drawn by the same attraction. If the author so writes as to violate this "esthetic distance," he is false to the canons of his art. But it is possible for a reader, too, to violate the "esthetic distance" by unintelligent reading of a book that keeps the distance very well indeed.

To illustrate this point of the attractiveness of sin, let me hark back once again to the original controversial book that occasioned this discussion. Many readers professed that they were shocked by the incident in *A Tree Grows in Brooklyn* in which the young girl's mother told her daughter that, speaking as a mother, she thought it would have been wrong for the daughter to spend the night with the young soldier she had met, but, speaking as a woman, she had to admit that it might have been beautiful. To be sure, no prudent mother would express her thought just that way to a young, impressionable girl, but actually *what* was said contains a profound truth—that there is in all wrongdoing (and not merely in sexual matters) an attractiveness and an allure that does appeal to our lower natures at the very time we realize that we must reprobate it.

One who does not realize the tremendous drawing power of evil, and especially evil that appeals primarily to our common sensuality, does not know life. Such a one is hardly equipped to appreciate literature. This is one fundamental reason why some books can be most rewarding for the mature reader, but a danger to the young, either in years or emotional development.

If one would care to examine a famous book in which this "esthetic distance" is not respected, there is no finer example than D. H. Lawrence's *Lady Chatterley's Lover*, which has recently risen to such lamentable prominence in this country because of the publication of the unexpurgated version and the decision of courts that the book is not "obscene." The following review appeared over my name in the June 6, 1959, issue of *America*. I think it will be evident that I am of the considered opinion that the minute detailing of sexual aberrations in the story is such that a normally sensitive reader is drawn into a sense of identification and sharing that is not merely an artistic trespass, but, for many a reader, a moral danger as well. I framed my judgment in the following terms:

Two reasons counsel an extended criticism of Lawrence's *Lady Chatterley's Lover*. This publication of the unexpurgated version of the novel has already stirred up a storm out of all proportion to the literary merits of Lawrence's last and, as is almost universally admitted, weakest novel. Second, the hearings now being conducted by the U. S. Post Office as to whether the obscenity of the book makes it unmailable bid fair to carry the book ultimately to the U. S. Supreme Court, where it will become a classic test case of "censorship."

The novel was first published in 1928 in Italy. It was sold clandestinely, mainly in the United States and England, was published in an expurgated version in both these countries, but never in its original form until this present publication by the Grove Press, a house that has for some time been specializing in "offbeat" literature. To be blunt about it, no U.S. publisher had dared to issue the complete work; Grove has now dared, and one wonders to what purpose.

For the book, despite the testimonials solicited from eminent literary figures, is simply not great literature, and that not merely because of the extremely frank passages which, it is charged, make the novel obscene. If the book did not carry the name of Lawrence, no one would bother too much about condemning or defending it.

The story is a mere sketch. Lady Chatterley is married to a man who has been rendered sexually impotent by wounds suffered in World War I. Their home is in one of England's industrial areas, and the young bride, revolted by the dehumanization of the mine and mill workers, and bored to death by the "intellectual" double talk of her husband and his upper-class cronies, begins to feel that the only way to achieve "fullness" in life lies in giving herself, utterly without reserve, to a real "man." She finds such a one in the gamekeeper on her husband's estate.

He is married to and separated from a shrewish wife. The story ends when Lady Chatterley announces to her husband that she is pregnant by the gamekeeper. At the close there is some indecision as to whether she and her paramour will get their divorces and settle down together—presumably in a foreign country. There are long, long passages of passionately detailed description of the physical liaison between the lovers. On these rest the charge that the book is obscene.

Though by no means a literary masterpiece, this work is without doubt seriously intended. Lawrence is revolted at the brutalization of man by the mine-pit and the stamping-machine and sincerely wants to register a protest. His book is saying that the life-forces manifest in the sex act are themselves becoming dehumanized. This he blames on the Victorian hush-hush attitude toward sex. It must be said at the same time, if we are to be fair, that Lawrence, as we know him through his letters, essays and personal life, was not a "dirty-minded lecher," as has been charged and will certainly now be repeated. He wrote strongly against "pornography" in literature (which he curiously distinguished from "obscenity"); he did not advocate sexual promiscuity; he was actually drawn to the Church because of its teaching on the sacramental nature of marriage.

But an author's intentions and how he dramatizes those intentions in a novel are two different things. Though Lawrence clearly wanted to shock people into what he apparently thought was a healthy attitude toward sex, the key questions remain: Was he justified in shocking them to this extent and, more important, was his attitude healthy?

I believe that the verdict must be that for general distribution this is an obscene book, not in the sense that Lawrence's intention was *ex professo* to corrupt, but in the sense that what he actually produced has a corrupting bent. Moreover, this bent of the total work appears in such explicit language in so many extended passages that Christian modesty, to say the least, impels us to rank this book with those that are restricted reading. They are so because, under the provisions of canon law, they *teach* immorality.

This aspect of teaching is all the more evident when one takes into consideration that Lawrence's attitudes toward sex were really the result of a fairly well-thought-out philosophy. He cultivated a mystique of sex which, to the Christian mind, is utterly pagan. Had he lived in the days of pagan Rome, one feels, Lawrence would have defended the "liturgical" character of some of the obscene religious rites, and he would have defended them with a religious fervor.

It is this crusading zeal that lifts this novel out of the slough of plain unadulterated dirty books. Unlike the works of a Mickey Spillane, this book does have something of social importance to say, but the way in which it says it becomes all the more misguiding because of the quasi-philosophy that adds to its allurement an air of profundity. Specialists, I believe, can handle this book. (May I interject that I *have*, and without harm to my ideals?) But the general reader, and especially those who have no sound principles on sex and marriage, could be profoundly disturbed. This is a prudential judgment which may be controverted in some quarters, but it is the only considered judgment I can make.

I believe that the same indictment can be leveled against Vladimir Nabokov's *Lolita*, which was published in the United States a year preceding *Lady Chatterley's Lover* and probably set the climate for the reception of the Lawrence shocker. In criticizing this book in the August 30, 1958, issue of *America*, I said:

This book, "proudly" published by G. P. Putnam's Sons (a feat that wins an accolade from a critic for its "courage"), is, without the slightest doubt in my mind, the most obscene lucubration to disgrace U.S. publishing in many a decade. The theme itself is distasteful enough: it concerns the perversions of a middle-aged European émigré who has an ineluctable fondness for what he calls "nymphets"—teen-age girls. The story deals in detail with his motel-to-motel dalliance with 12-year-old Lolita, who, to be frank about it, is a spoiled, even vicious, sexually precocious brat.

The details are, as one critic opines, "quite delicately" treated; that is to say, there are none of the "obscene" four-letter words. It is all very sophisticated, dripping with phony "culture," written in an arch style that pleads for "understanding." But it is weary, cynical, degenerate and, precisely because of its veneer of blasé charm, emits more noisesomely than a cruder tale would the nauseating odor of festering lilies. Incidentally, it proves admirably the wise dictum that "only the truly vulgar don't see that pornography is utterly boring."

These considerations on objectionable parts and total effect, and on a recognition of sin for what (at the very least, to some appreciable degree) it is lead us to a final aspect, that of the extent to which descriptions of sin may be detailed without violation of either artistic or moral canons. The above remarks on *Lady Chatterley's Lover* and *Lolita* could perhaps have been equally well incorporated in the following chapter, for the various elements in our moral norms are almost inextricably intertwined, for literature—or a good book, if you prefer the concrete to the abstract—is an organic thing. But criticism of a good (or a bad) book, though it must also be organic—of a piece—does have to divide to conquer.

With this brief apology for an unavoidable amount of overlapping, let's take the next step in essaying our moral norms.

4. Detailed Description of Sin

THE SECOND principle for consideration in this matter of sin in literature rests on the truth that an author has a further responsibility than that of portraying sin as sin in at least the minimum sense we have been considering. By the mere fact that he disseminates his views for general consumption, the author assumes this further responsibility. He makes himself liable to the charge or open to the compliment that he has been the occasion of harm or of advantage to thousands of his readers. He cannot disown this responsibility, for literature does not exist in a vacuum—it is for human consumption, and human beings react in a human, that is to say, in a morally justifiable or unjustifiable manner. It follows, then, that although an author may comment or discuss sin in a way that is basically defensible, he soon finds that he is faced with the further problem: how explicitly may he describe sinful actions? It is perhaps almost inevitable that sensual sin here springs to mind as the prime example. It is almost inevitable because sensual sin is of its nature the most seductive and alluring, if not always the most serious. But this is not the only sin to which I refer in this discussion. A novel that would portray, with explicit and attractive descriptions, the rise to power of a clever and unscrupulous big-businessman, for example, might merit even stronger condemnation than the sexy novel, because of the fact that its immoral impact might well be more insidious because less easily discernible.

How explicitly, then, may sin be described? Here we have the second of the general principles that have to guide critic and reader. The principle may be formulated thus: sin, though recognized for what it is, may never be so described as to become a proximate temptation to sin for a normally well-balanced reader. This principle is immutably true; its application, however, as hinted above, is so variable that it is extremely difficult to apply as a general objective and immutable norm.

It is difficult of application, not because the moral principle governing occasions of sin is misty, but because the human imagination, upon which literature plays, is so variable a factor. A description that is vividly disturbing for one reader may leave another reader quite unmoved; a mere word or phrase may shock some while others take it in stride. This is the source of much of the controversy that has raged over many good and even great books, such as Sigrid Undset's, Graham Greene's, François Mauriac's. Both sides, those who condemned, and those who defended, were undoubtedly equally moral and equally zealous in upholding moral standards, but the responsiveness and bent of their own imagination inevitably colored their reaction.

This latent power of evoking a trend of thought or a train of imagination is something that literature, far from trying to avoid, must of its nature exercise. It is of the very nature of art to suggest, to lead the mind and imagination on to exploring realms that the mere word or phrase only passingly reveals. If some minds run on too quickly, too vividly, to fill in the suggested outlines (and that readiness may rise from many causes, ranging from a natural lovely delicateness of sensibility to downright prudishness) must the critic, striving to judge the book for the average reader, condemn it out of hand because of the relatively few who may so react?

This step of my thought may seem, I know, to be backward; it would seem that we have already considered this aspect of the problem earlier, when we discussed whether or not objectionable parts in a book necessarily demand that the whole book be condemned. There is some overlapping, but the distinction is that the earlier consideration was concerned with the *quantity* of such passages; here we are considering rather the *quality*.

There are, of course, limits here that any normal person will immediately recognize and respect. A book that is obviously and studiedly obscene does not fall within this discussion, for it has by the very fact of its patent obscenity cut itself off from the normal, common attitudes of human life which are the raw stuff of literature and art. And, as a matter of fact, such books would seldom be a temptation to the normally discriminating reader (if he read them) because, as a critic has aptly remarked, the fact "that they are infinitely boring will seem a paradox only to the adolescent and the truly vulgar." Certainly only the adolescent and the truly vulgar could in any serious way whatever be tempted by the coy obscenities that pullulate in such atrocities as *Forever Amber*, *The Manatee* and *Caroline Chérie*. Does any serious lover of books even remember these literary spooks?

Or does the critic fulfill his obligation both as a critic and moral guide (the two functions are not necessarily disparate; they are rather complementary) if he praises what other excellencies there are and still warns that the perhaps too vivid passages lie in wait to trap the too impressionable reader? This, of course, was the problem a conscientious critic faced, perhaps most delicately, in his approach to Greene's *The End of the Affair*. I think the reviewer does fulfill his function in simply issuing the necessary warning. If the objection is raised that praise of an otherwise excellent book amounts to condonation or approval of the temptation that *may* confront the reader, it would seem to betray that proper weight was not given to the cautionary phrases the critic was at pains to employ.

A critic, then, cannot go further than the premises allow. This is especially true if the critic be one charged in a special way with some responsibility for the spiritual well-being of those who depend on his judgment. Such a critic cannot indiscriminately say of every book that contains a vivid passage that is a possible temptation: "This is a bad book and no one can read it without moral infection." Such a verdict runs the great danger of forming false consciences, of occasioning sin where perhaps in all honesty there would have been no sin if the flat verdict had not rashly alerted too impressionable consciences. The critic may indeed say, and may have to say, "This is a dubious book and I would advise you to pass it by." The prospective reader may be imprudent or rash or silly if he doesn't heed the advice, but whether or not he will sin because of the passages at issue in the book can be determined only within the sanctity of his own conscience.

Does this attitude seem to be a masterpiece of straddling and inconclusiveness? It will seem so, I think, only to those who have not realized that in the individual application of moral principles there are relatively few cases that are clearly black or clearly white.

Is this to hold that what may be a temptation to one may not be a temptation to another? Or that what is a temptation today may not be one tomorrow? Yes, definitely. And this is by no means moral relativism. It is simply an application of the principle that the circumstances surrounding an act are one of the elements that determine the act's morality. To take an example: indecent exposure is always, anywhere and for everyone, a proximate occasion of sin. But when is exposure indecent? When style decrees that skirts should be seventeen inches from the ground? Or is it eighteen? Or is a modest bathing suit on the beach enough to constitute a modest gown on the dance floor?

Perhaps much of this attitude which demands from the critic a black or white answer rises from the fact that too many readers think that the critic's function is to solve all such problems. The critic cannot solve the problem for every reader, as I shall discuss later in the chapter on creative reading. Each reader must in a sense be his own Index as he reads. This is his personal moral obligation and no one can relieve him of it. If by some happenstance the Pope or a Bishop were heartily to recommend a book and the individual reader found that it was a definite moral danger to him, he would be obliged to stop reading—no matter who had recommended it. We might expect, however, that he would not immediately accuse those who recommended it of lax judgment, but would simply say to himself, "Well, I'm just not attuned to that sort of book." Nor need this reader feel hurt or abashed. All it means is simply that his sensibilities, whether higher or lower, are not of the same wave length as the sensibilities of those who commended the book.

There is another observation that seems in place here. Scenes can be handled in such a fashion that, even without explicit and detailed suggestive treatment, they may build up to a pervasive moral danger. It is sometimes not precisely the fullness of the description so much as the explicitness and clarity of the impression left that may give rise to this. The very fact that art influences the imagination by suggestion, as we have said, gives it this tremendous power. A scene, accordingly, that is insistently hinted at and whose flavor seasons whole passages and perhaps the entire book, though it never emerges in shocking and brutal details, may, without being a specific temptation, become a source of infection because of its constantly felt presence. There are not a few books in any given year which, though they cannot be flatly called pornographic, do have to be castigated as generally unhealthy. In this category I would most unhesitatingly place most of John O'Hara's work, notably his *From the Terrace*, and James Gould Cozzens' *By Love Possessed*.

The principle, then, holds good: sin may never be treated, whether explicitly or by suggestion, so as to be a source of proximate temptation to the normally adjusted reader—nor may a critic lose sight of this principle in passing judgment on the book. To be sure, the application of the principle is sometimes a delicate job, for on the one side lies laxity in moral judgment and on the other side the danger of forming false consciences. Indeed, the critic finds a rather smug and uncomfortable position forced upon him, for he must presume (must he not?) that *he* is the normally adjusted or discriminating reader. "All the world is queer save thee and me, and even thou . . ."

If we put together these two principles we have been discussing—namely, that sin must be recognized for what it is and may never be so treated as to become a temptation—we come to an interesting conclusion. It is that the reviewer of the book and the reader of the review and of the book share a mutual responsibility. The reviewer is accountable for the moral and artistic soundness of the judgments which impelled him to commend the book to those he thought were discriminating enough, mature and balanced enough, not to be seduced by a phrase, a scene. The reviewer is also accountable for issuing a sufficient caution to indicate that for some such a danger may exist.

The reader's responsibility consists in this: if he knows from experience or prudently suspects that almost any description of sin will be a trouble to him, then he has the duty of reading the cautionary remarks in a review with more than average care to note the caution. This relationship between reviewer and reader will be at once sensible and mutually advantageous. It will forestall the reader's readiness immediately to suspect the reviewer of fostering immorality, of "recommending" bad books. On the other hand it will enable the reviewer to write with a fair and confident assurance that he will really be understood when he endorses a book for mature audiences. There are some readers, of course, who would demand of the reviewer, and particularly of the Catholic reviewer, bare categorical statements that a book is simply "good" or "bad." They are of this uncomplicated frame of mind with regard to literature largely because they feel, as they say, that judgments on books *must* be severe in order to keep controversial books out of the hands of children who are today, we are told, so eager to take advantage of every moral leeway. To such an attitude there is, I think, but one answer—the critic who is dealing with adult literature cannot in all conscience be expected to assume a function that is the responsibility of the parents of impressionable children.

5. Fiction and the Art of Living

THE QUESTION of morality in literature, with special emphasis on fiction, must be discussed and decided, it seems to me, on such principles as those stated above. Much more, of course, could be said by way of theory, but for practical purposes I believe that further discussion would descend to finespun distinctions.

I would like to go on now to discuss a point that often touches upon the subject of morality but which is in essence a question of the novelist's proper function *as* a novelist. The novelist, like any artist, is dealing with two basic but imponderable realities—truth and beauty. The adequacy or the excellence with which he blends these two elements will to a large extent determine his stature in the world of literature. For he *must* blend the two: if there is no basic truth in his work, its appeal to the reader's heart and mind is spurious; if there is no perceptible beauty, there is no possible engagement of the emotions. It follows, moreover, that a proper realization of the respective function of these two elements will to a great extent determine the justice of the reader's demands on the author.

What can the reader demand of the author? He can and must demand, as the present discussion has endeavored to show, that the author treat human beings as human beings and human life as human life—in other words that he never portray men as either angels or fiends incarnate. The reader can further demand and must demand that in treating human life humanly the author does not so glamorize the sinful element in his characters as to run the risk of making the reader's own life less human. But (and here is the point of departure for this further analysis) the reader has no right to demand that the author teach him *how* to live. (We are speaking of fiction, let it be recalled; *some* books, of course, are written with the precise and express purpose of "teaching" how to live.)

The reader cannot reasonably, and therefore should not, go to fiction *primarily for instruction.* This statement seems so self-evident as to need no explanation. I think, however, that much of the difficulty felt by many who conceive that most modern novels are just not worth reading springs precisely from a quite complete forgetfulness or ignorance of the fact that all literature, and fiction above all, is written primarily to give pleasure and not to impart instruction. A letter occasioned by the famous *Tree* revealed (with unconscious humor) this erroneous point of view, when the lady correspondent stated (referring to an amusing, if somewhat crude passage on this subject in Miss Smith's novel) that if she "ever wanted to find out how to wean a baby daughter [she] would go to a standard manual for mothers or to her doctor and not to Betty Smith." Precisely, and so would I, were such a happy status possible for me. The point is, however, that such an attitude in a reader casts upon any author a burden that is unfair and overwhelming. Miss Smith, Graham Greene, Henry Morton Robinson, any author you can mention, never, if he is a novelist and not a mere propagandist, sets out to *teach* us in the pages of a novel how children ought to be raised, how married life ought to be lived, how education should be conducted and so on. What the author wants to say simply is that this is how and why his characters actually did live, this is actually how and why they did get educated or succeed or fail in marriage. There is, to be sure, an "oughtness" involved in this, as we shall see, but its overt inculcation is not the prime and formal function of literature.

Is the conclusion to be drawn, then, that we learn nothing from fiction? Is the reading of fiction merely "escapism," time

71

wasted that adds nothing to the fullness of human life? By no means, and if fiction—I am obviously speaking of serious fiction and not of the silly little boy-meets-girl romance of the slick magazines—is really read, the reader does learn something, but he learns in the way that is art's unique way—he learns through pleasure; he glimpses truth through the windows of beauty. And if he does so strike upon something beautiful let him have no fears that he is missing truth, for truth and beauty are but different facets of the same reality.

But here is the rub. "We grant you," the chorus of dissent would chant, "we grant you that no one who reads sensibly should go to novelists to be instructed; we will be content merely to find the truth of fact. But where, where in the world in so much modern fiction, can you point out to us any slightest vestige of beauty?"

Let me try to answer the question by a few concrete examples. When I reviewed Marquand's *So Little Time* in *America* for August 28, 1943, I did so in terms of fairly high praise. Some readers of the book, however, would have been inclined to agree with the review by Isabel Patterson which appeared in the *Herald Tribune Books* for December 26, 1943. Her judgment ran:

> Nobody in the story had any truths, ideas to orient themselves by. There is not a trace of intellectual activity in the characters; they do not think, therefore they do not feel anything but a rather dull discomfort and boredom. . . . *So Little Time* is a group portrait of people in a huddle, wondering what for. . . .

If that were the complete picture, then there would not be the dimmest glimmer of beauty in *So Little Time*. But, strange as it may seem, there is a certain beauty to be discovered. If it was not consciously written into the book, it nevertheless emerges from the book. It results from what we might call the "overtones" of the novel. It vibrates in the whole poignant contrast which the author never points up explicitly but which trembles on every page. It is the contrast between what his "huddled" people are in the story and what their very lack hints they could have been. Here is where the beauty of the story lies. It is the beauty of the potentiality of the human soul, unrealized, frustrated and dissipated in these particular characters, but still fundamentally and eternally there. This is the "oughtness" we shall treat later.

It is through these hints of a dimly suggested beauty that the author actually does, though it may not have been his conscious intention, set before us "our endless search for the good in human experience"—and so, in a sense, does teach a deep lesson. But if I approach the book with the primary expectation and demand that the author give me instruction in the art and goals of living, I ask him to assume a responsibility that is not his, the responsibility of being a moral guide. He cannot, indeed, be an *immoral* guide, but the truth he hints at and suggests cannot in a novel be pinned down by a blackboard-and-pointer method—it must emerge from the beauty of the characters, of the situation, of the overtones. A similar discovery of beauty in apparently unlikely places is to be found in the works of Graham Greene. The message, if we may use that disliked word, in *The Power and the Glory*, the oblique statement of what the book has to say, is that the priesthood is glorious and deathless. The lives of the two priests in the book, the protagonist "whiskey-priest" and the secondary character, Padre José, who is living a "married" life in the village, are a running commentary on their own realization of the sublimity of the vocation to which they have been false.

There must be at least this gleam of reflected beauty in any great art and in literary art particularly, for without it the truth contained will never be more than the mere truth of fact, it will never be the truth of ideal. When the truth of mere fact is informed by this reflection of beauty, then the truth of ideal can spring from the wedding of the two. Geoffrey Wilson's love affair (which does not trespass on the moral principles treated above) in *So Little Time* is a truth of fact—here is something that did happen, in the imaginative world of the author's mind, of course—but it is much more than merely that. Informed and suffused with the author's own oblique commentary on the emptiness of Geoffrey's life, the episode merges into a suggestion of an ideal, namely, that the closeness and sharing of marriage would have been Geoffrey Wilson's salvation had he only known how to achieve them. Francie Nolan's experience with the pervert in *A Tree Grows in Brooklyn* was a truth of fact, but transformed by the author's appreciation of the young girl's instinctive modesty and of her mother's protective love, even such a realistic scene takes on the glow of the truth of an ideal.

A similar suffusion of the truth of fact by the truth of ideal is to be discovered in Greene's *The End of the Affair,* and here, indeed, the process by which stated fact is elevated to implied ideal is almost explicit. It is the woman's (Sarah's) realization that there is an ideal of love for which she has been reaching blindly and mistakenly that brings her, with God's grace, to the shattering knowledge that the love she has been adulterously enjoying is empty and degrading.

This truth can be discovered in many a current novel. To mention but a few, some glow of an ideal can be discerned beneath the mere external facts in such novels as John Phillips' *The Second Happiest Day,* Ruth Park's *The Witch's Thorn,* Gladys Schmitt's *Confessors of the Name.* In still other works the ideal does not merely glimmer—it blazes with all-suffusing light in such great novels as H. F. M. Prescott's *The Man on a Donkey* and in such good ones as Charles A. Brady's *Stage of Fools,* Charles Bracelen Flood's *Love Is a Bridge,* L. P. Hartley's *My Fellow Devils,* and *God's Frontier,* by José Martin Descalzo.

The psychological fact of the matter is that truth is of necessity an element in intellectual pleasure. I cannot take a legitimate intellectual pleasure in something that I know to be intellectually or morally false. Literature, dealing with human life, must deal with facts and their interpretation, their meaning and bearing. Literature will teach; it cannot help it. But it must never *seem* to be teaching. And the reader must not approach it with the presumption or hope that it will, as its primary function, impart instruction. It would perhaps be better, instead of saying that literature does teach, to say that the reader actually will learn, though literature does not specifically instruct.

Here a practical difficulty is posed for critics—and especially for Catholic critics. If the critic felt with adequate assurance that all his readers already knew sufficiently well how to conduct the business of life and were going to fiction, not for a blueprint of how to live, but for an enlargement of their own views and lives, either by way of confirmation or contrast, then the critic would be able to assess the work more objectively, without the uneasy feeling that he had to be issuing constant warnings. Since some, however, apparently do read fiction under the impression that it is going to instruct them how to live, the critic must sometimes temper his purely critical judgment with a regard for practical prudence. But it would be totally unfair to expect that such a regard for practical prudence will be plenary enough to forestall the possibility of any and all demurrers.

Truth, then, must be one of the constituent elements of a novel, but it alone does not *make* a novel; it is essential but artistically secondary. It is subordinate to and presupposed by the fact that the aim of art is to give pleasure. But it is so important that if falsehood, if untruth, constitute a large or essential portion of the burden of the story, the story fails *as art*, no matter what the specious pleasure derived. For though the end of art is to please it must please according to the rule of right reason.

This is why the writing of a serious historical novel is an exacting task. The author has to keep two truths clearly before him. First, there is the truth of historical fact, which he may indeed embellish and expand but which he can never contravene. Second, he has to keep before him the truth of ideal, which he shares in common with the purely imaginative writer. In the historical novel, this is often reducible to a psychological problem—the justice and perception with which the author catches and projects the "feel" of the time. Such books as Lloyd Douglas' *The Robe* and Sholem Asch's *The Apostle, Mary* and *Moses*, all fail under either or both of these aspects because they deny at least by implication the truth of certain historical occurrences or distort the psychological picture of the past. The pleasure they give, therefore, is in so far an illegitimate pleasure. The same must be the verdict on the ambitiously conceived *The Sinner of Saint Ambrose*, by Robert Raynolds. The magnificently conceived and executed *The Man on a Donkey*, by H. F. M. Prescott, in contrast, is true to all known historical facts and suffused, in addition, with the even more important truth of the spiritual ideal that animated the Pilgrimage of Grace to rise in protest against Henry VIII's confiscation of the monasteries.

The purely imaginative writer is spared this double risk. The truth of the facts portrayed in his book depends on his own creation. The bickerings of Father Chisholm and the Mother Superior in *The Keys of the Kingdom* actually happened in the author's heart and mind; the critic or reader cannot dismiss them by saying "these things don't happen" because he thinks their portrayal is regrettable. The protracted adulterous affair in Greene's *The End of the Affair* is a thing that definitely took place in Greene's artistic imagination; again the critic or reader cannot dismiss it because he is rightly convinced that the occurrence of such affairs in real life is lamentable. The purely imaginative author, of course, is also bound by the demands of a psychological verisimilitude as well. The facts that he invents have not merely to ring true in themselves; they must be linked into a rational pattern that is logical and plausible.

Here again we verge onto the inescapable question of individual taste. Though the formal purpose of art be to give legitimate pleasure, not every work of art is going to please everyone. You may simply not like a certain type of book. Grim, tragic stories unrelieved by any slightest bit of sweetness and light may not appeal to you, but that of itself is no proof that the book is not a work of art. If it can be pointed out—and this is the critic's job—that the book does contain the elements of truth and beauty that we have been discussing, then the novel will be objectively a work of art, whether this particular reader derives pleasure from it or not. The whole point of this discussion has not by any means been to bludgeon people into feeling obliged to like certain things because a critic happens to like them. It has rather been to discuss some general principles on which tastes can be properly built and refined, and judgments by both critics and readers more sanely and helpfully issued.

That there is need of such temperate discussion among Catholics has been but too sadly proved by the openly intemperate tone of some of the correspondence occasioned by reviews of the books we have been mentioning. Catholic reviewers who have spoken appreciatively of men like Graham Greene are not too infrequently told that they are doing the devil's work by recommending pornographic literature. Such unobjective judgment, such one-sided criticism (if it may be dignified by that name), when engaged publicly in a discussion of current fiction, leads to the suspicion that many Catholic readers do not really know the function either of literature or of literary criticism. It leads to the further suspicion that there are Catholic bigots, too.

It is not in this fashion that we are going to influence modern literary thought, whether through creation or through criticism. There is no question here of yielding the outposts to the children of this world. Here is a matter of knowing principles clearly and holding them tenaciously but of being temperate and judicious in applying them. Catholic critics and readers must, if they are to influence literary thought, begin and continue, with God's help, to read and judge books in this fashion.

PART II
"REALISM" AND
MORAL EVALUATION

"Realism" and Moral Evaluation

A GREAT DEAL of the confusion that exists among readers as to the moral acceptability of a book is occasioned by some misapprehensions over the word "realism." Many people are under the impression that to call a novel "realistic" is *ipso facto* to stigmatize it as pornographic. When the storm of controversy began to gather around Graham Greene's *The Heart of the Matter*, for instance, a great number of people who objected to the book seem to have based their objections on the simple charge that the novel was "realistic."

This may seem to be merely a matter of semantics, but it goes deeper than that. Catholic critics and readers, I suppose, have clear in their own minds just what they themselves mean when they use the term "realistic." The question, however, is whether what they mean is what the term ought to mean and actually has meant in the history and customs of criticism.

The word "realism" is not, as a matter of fact, a very operative word. Of itself it says very little and its meaning in literary criticism is by no means as clear as it is in philosophy. It is generally, in its literary application, used as opposed to idealism, but, as we shall see, such a distinction does not always indicate a clear-cut difference. An investigation of the use of the word through the labyrinths of literary criticism will reveal that its fundamental meaning boils down practically to "objectivity." The realistic author is one who takes his data from the real life about him and who fashions that data into his story, into his work of art, with a minimum of intrusion and influence by his own subjective ideas and opinions.

Another way of saying the same thing, perhaps, is to say

that the realistic writer is one who sets himself the goal of telling the whole truth as it is demanded by his subject matter. It is in this sense, for example, that recent hagiographers have been realists. Too many of their predecessors had been idealists, in the sense that they exercised a not too fair selectivity, but we are now more and more being shown the whole saint with his defects, passions and human weaknesses, together with his heroic virtue. In other words, we get the real saint and not a sugared facsimile of him.

In this sense of telling all the truth the subject matter requires for its adequate presentation, every great author in the world and every good literary craftsman can be said to be a realist. Dickens, for example, tells us the truth about London slums, about the debtors' prisons, the poorhouses and the whole Industrial Revolution, in sufficient detail to give adequate foundation for the truth he is at pains to demonstrate. Dickens is, of course, at the same time a very subjective writer in the sense that his own imagination and sympathy and scorn suffuse every page. But no author can ever be utterly objective, and particularly in fiction the author's subjective slant will not invalidate the objectivity so long as it does not positively distort the true reporting of the subject matter. If Dickens' sympathy for England's Oliver Twists led him into sentimental exaggeration, as it frequently did, then in so far he is not realistic. If, on the other hand, this sympathy impelled him to paint all the more truly, because he wrote with sincere and solid emotion, then his subjective reactions helped make him all the more a true realist.[1]

[1] Those who may be surprised at my including Dickens among the "realistic" writers may be interested and, perhaps, somewhat persuaded of the soundness of the inclusion by the following passage from *Sigrid Undset: a Study in Christian Realism*, by A. H. Winsnes (Sheed & Ward, 1953). "Sigrid Undset is the Christian realist *par excellence*. More than any other writer she gathers together the threads

The fictional character, therefore, must have the truth about him told adequately by his creator. That adequacy will be determined by many things—by the author's conception of the type of character he is, by the times in which he is made to live, by his social environment, by his friends and comrades, by his work and so on. Given this complex pattern into which the character is to fit, the author must tell enough truth about that pattern to bring it to life and make it a real world that will hold together consistently and so be convincing.

"As much truth as is demanded by the subject matter"— that, I believe, is the real test of sane realism.[2] If more factual details than necessary for the portrayal of the character and the development of the story are presented, the author will be open to the charge of overwriting or of propagandizing and

---

of the European realist position. Her writing has grown organically out of the powerful presentation of everyday reality which we meet in the nineteenth-century novel and which is the essence of literary realism. But the preconditions go back further in time, to Shakespeare and his contemporaries and to Chaucer. 'One thinks of Dickens when one reads Chaucer,' she writes, '. . . they are closely related, both were realists who described the actuality they found before them—and it was a better actuality than we can find'" (pp. 8–9). The soundness of the realistic approach to literature, as we are here considering it, may be pointed out by the further remark of Mr. Winsnes that Sigrid Undset was determined to treat even the relationship of creatures to the Creator "as a fact just as realistic as any erotic impulse or longing for earthly happiness."

[2] It may be of some interest to quote at this point from a letter received from Graham Greene after I had asked for his comments on the four articles on realism as they originally appeared in *America*. Mr. Greene wrote, in part: "The only point at which I felt some doubt was in your first article when you refer to 'as much truth as is demanded by the subject matter' and went on to refer to 'if more truth than that is presented the author would be open to the charge of over-writing, of propaganda,' but I found as I went on with your series of articles that I had misunderstood your meaning, with which I am in complete agreement."

preaching. If insufficient factual details are given, something like a lack of motivation, of unreality or inadequacy will flaw the work.

If realism fundamentally means, then, that the author approaches his material with the determination to tell the truth about it and the truth as seen in real life, the word itself has not advanced our thinking very much. But at least it ought thus far to be evident that there is no need to flinch and blench when you may hear that this or that book is realistic. The blenching and the flinching may indeed be justified, but only after you have put a further question. This is the further and important question: what kind of realism? I believe that realism should be considered, so to speak, as a *genus*, subdivided into two divisions or *species*. These two divisions will be called naturalistic and idealistic. Realism can be so subdivided, as it were, because it is simply a technique, a way of doing things—in literature, a way of writing. It is not a way of thinking. And it is only when realism is employed under the influence of a particular bent of mind that it takes on something of the character of an ideology. A man may, accordingly, be a realist who writes realistically from either a naturalistic or an idealistic climate of thought.

What, then, is a "naturalistic realist"? Such a writer, because he maintains that he is a realist, will claim that he is actually telling the whole truth his subject matter demands. But because he is also a naturalist or thinks (all unconsciously perhaps) along the lines of naturalism, he cannot, as a matter of fact, tell that whole truth. He cannot, because naturalism is that habit of mind (conscious and articulated, or vaguely instinctive) which either denies or refuses to consider the existence of suprasensible realities—those realities which we very aptly call the imponderables, the intangibles. This is but to say that a naturalist is a positivist who by definition will admit the

84

existence of no values that cannot be examined and weighed by the senses—or, as he would say, subjected to "scientific measurement." What he can see and feel, touch, hear and smell —these are the things that have ascertainable value. All the rest can have no value or, if perhaps theoretically they may have a value, it is really not worth considering because we cannot in practice know what the value is.

The naturalist, accordingly, will attach no importance to spiritual realities, and when I say "spiritual" I do not necessarily mean "religious." There are many spiritual truths, facts, realities, which are not of their nature specifically religious, though frequently their finest flowering will burgeon only when their ground is religious. Such, for example, are the virtues of patriotism, of love and reverence, of honor. Such, too (and indeed it is a spiritual reality that is particularly subject to the naturalist's denial), is compunction or remorse, and the whole gamut of those spiritual realities covered by what we call the dictates of conscience.[3]

[3] A very perceptive discussion of mid-nineteenth-century realism, especially as evident in the pioneering work of Zola, commonly regarded as the father of literary realism, is contained in *Literary Criticism: A Short History*, by William K Wimsatt, Jr., and Cleanth Brooks (Knopf, 1957, pp. 456 ff.). What is of particular interest here is the rapidity with which realism "quickly intensified into the phase called 'naturalism'" (p. 457). The quotation from Zola (p. 458) is particularly instructive as giving the basic creed of naturalistic realists:
"What matters most to me is purely naturalistic, purely psychological. Instead of having principles (royalism, Catholicism) I shall have laws (heredity, atavism). . . I am satisfied to be a scientist, to tell of that which exists, while seeking the underlying reasons. . . . A simple exposé of the facts of a family by showing the interior mechanism which directs them."
The authors then append a treatment of the rise of naturalism in America, with special emphasis on the work of Frank Norris. They end with the wry conclusion that "naturalism . . . was contemporary and socially didactic. But whether it was in any very strict sense 'natural' or 'true,' or scientifically real or true, might all along have

This naturalistic bent in a great deal of modern realistic writing can often be discovered in the author's attitude toward free will. The naturalistic writer will deny its existence—not, of course, in explicit terms as a doctrine to be refuted, but implicitly in and through his characters' actions. A very good analysis of this trait of naturalism has been essayed by J. Donald Adams in his column, "Speaking of Books," in the New York *Times* Book Review. Mr. Adams was contrasting *The Naked and the Dead*, by Norman Mailer, and Graham Greene's *The Heart of the Matter*, which, as I have remarked, has been unjustly castigated in many quarters as being realistic in a derogatory sense. Mr. Adams found that the Mailer book, with its deadening insistence on the vast and sullenly overwhelming social forces that pushed the protagonist into the war, sent him to the front and plunged him into dangers and deviltries, gave the inescapable impression that the young man was not personally responsible for his actions. Society, the war, environment, what you will, was the sinner; the wrong-doing GI was swept willy-nilly along with the stream.

But Scobie, Graham Greene's character, sins and knows that he is sinning. It is his personal actions—chosen deliberately, their consequences foreseen (if only *in confuso*, as the theologians would say)—which charge the book on every page with a realization of personal responsibility. In this sense, then, if in no other, *The Heart of the Matter* is quite definitely not a naturalistic book. No naturalistic novel can ever be so explicit in its affirmation of the free, self-determining human will. This same enlightening contrast stands out boldly in such more recent novels as *From Here to Eternity* and *The End of the Affair*, in *From the Terrace* and *My Fellow Devils*.

---

been considered another question—with obvious embarrassments to an affirmative answer."

In other words, as our further discussion may bring out, a confirmed literary naturalist (but not necessarily a realist) almost automatically cuts himself off from a whole field of reality.

The early days of realism in American literature provide proof, I believe, of the soundness of this position, namely that realism is a *genus* which is divided into two *species* through the operation of the specific difference of the underlying philosophy. Realism did not, in its American beginnings, manifest any inherent suggestiveness or degeneracy; above all it was not unduly fascinated by matters of sex. This becomes evident when we consider the works of such men as William Dean Howells. He is acknowledged to be one of the fathers of the realistic movement in American letters, and yet it has been pointed out by almost all critics that his novels are reticent practically to the point of prudery about anything that has even a remote bearing on sex. It took quite a while (at a slower pace in American literature than in French, probably because of our lingering Puritan heritage) for this initial realistic technique to succumb to the influence of a frank and easily discernible naturalistic trend of thought. Howells and most of his contemporary partners in this "new" realistic school would very likely hold up their hands in holy horror if they were alive today to read such works as *The Naked and the Dead, From Here to Eternity*, all of Farrell, Caldwell, O'Hara and the like, and to hear it said that this type of writing is but a logical and inevitable development of the realism they had injected into American letters.

How did such a development come about? It came about because, while realism as a literary technique was being experimented with by American authors, the naturalistic thinking of two men in particular began to influence those authors. These two men were Herbert Spencer, the English social scientist, as we would probably call him today, and Charles Darwin, the biologist and propagandist for his conception of evolution. Whether or not the novelists who began to write naturalistically ever made an explicit study of Spencer and

Darwin is beside the point. Whether they studied or not, they were nevertheless absorbing Spencer's and Darwin's attitude toward life and values as it was reflected in the cultural atmosphere all around them. As a matter of fact, however, Dreiser, to name but one, had read extensively in Spencer, and his realistic technique ran more and more in the channels of naturalistic thought.

Further, far from being any logical and necessary development of realism, the naturalistic frame of mind actually results in a denial of the very realism professed. The naturalist, in denying or at least belittling implicitly or explicitly the reality of suprasensible values, is automatically cut off from telling as much truth about his subject matter as that matter may very likely demand. The whole field of spiritual truth, for instance, is forbidden the naturalist by his underlying philosophy. Realizing or feeling uneasy that he is not telling the whole truth in this sector, he will almost inevitably be impelled, as a sort of compensation, to heap up too many facts in another sector and this will lead, as I have suggested, to the double fault of overwriting and lack of motivation. Perhaps the best way to explain or develop this thought is by example. The best example that comes to mind is the character of Grace Tate in John O'Hara's *A Rage to Live.* Much the same could be said of Prewitt in Jones' *From Here to Eternity* or of Alfred Eaton in O'Hara's *From the Terrace.*

Grace is quite a sinner and her sins are the stock in trade that characterizes much of this type of writing: her sins are those of adolescent experimentation in sex, and later, of marital infidelity. But O'Hara does not and indeed cannot portray her as a credible, a believable sinner. Nowhere, before, during or after her aberrations is there the slightest indication of hesitancy, of reluctance to yield to temptation, of distaste, of regret or remorse. Her feelings are unmotivated. The subsequent tenor of her life is serene and unruffled (at least within her own self— she does lose the love of her husband). The point is that O'Hara is forced by naturalism to present his character in this way, for he believes (as far as the man may be judged through his writing) that the existence of any imperatives of conscience, of moral law, of any ethical, and much more, of any religious and supernatural standards, is something that is chimerical, or if not that unreal, at least something of no great importance.

It may be, of course, that here and there among the millions of people in the world there are some who sin blindly, almost automatically, instinctively and with a carefree heart. But such a person is a moral cretin. And as far as the uses of literature go, such a person is simply not interesting as a character. An author who makes such a character the central figure of his novel by the very fact bars whole realms of true reality from his consideration. Real life is not lived that way.

The naturalist writer cannot, therefore, from this viewpoint, tell as much of the truth as his subject matter, real life, demands. He is in this respect less than a realist.

On the other hand the naturalist will err by excess. He will carry his realism to the point of propaganda. This he will do by an inartistic and wearying amassing of details. We may grant that it is necessary for a James T. Farrell to tell us that Studs Lonigan wallowed not too infrequently in drunken orgies. But once this has been said and described, there is no need to repeat the detailed description every time a similar scene occurs. Not only is there no need, but the very repetition becomes by its dogged insistence a factor of imbalance. It belabors the truth more than is demanded for the presentation of the subject matter and so becomes unreal. This same obsession with details vitiates much of the work of Robert Penn Warren, especially his latest novel, *The Cave*. It may conceivably be true that the hillbillies of Tennessee are as sex-ridden as this book makes them out to be, but Warren's constant harping on the theme results in an atmosphere of unreality. A critical judgment in such circumstances finds itself inevitably recalling Aristotle's dictum about possible improbabilities and impossible probabilities.

A remark that was illuminating in a sense certainly not intended by the critic was made in a review of Jones' *From Here to Eternity*. Admitting the frequency with which Jones makes use of the famous four-letter words in the novel, the critic went on to say that after the first few pages the monotonous frequency began to act on the reader as a sort of rhythmic accompaniment, a pulsing undertone that was devoid of meaning and served only to accent the pace of the story. The illumination that was perhaps unconsciously shed is this: here is one of the inevitable results of a raw naturalism. The insistence on details finally robs those details of the power to shock, and since that was the only power they originally had, they lose all significance. It is certainly small critical praise to accord a novel to say that a good percentage of its wordage is devoid of meaning. Style, we had always been led to believe, is concerned with the discriminating use of significant words.

The naturalist, accordingly, deviates from true realism first of all by defect—the cardinal defect of not seeing human nature whole. Then, feeling perhaps all unconsciously dissatisfied with what he begins to suspect is a partial picture, he attempts to strengthen its weakness by an overaccumulation of purely sensible details. And this leads to the second fault, one of excess. On two counts, therefore, the naturalist is not, and cannot be, a true realist.

At this point, it would seem that I have reached a contradiction. If naturalism does entail such a twofold betrayal of true realism, then such a thing as a naturalistic realism would contain mutually repugnant elements—it would be a contradiction in terms. This is true in theory and indeed the contradiction can be discovered to some degree in those naturalists who push their philosophy to extreme application. As a matter of fact, as Horton and Edwards point out in their *Backgrounds of American Literary Thought* (Appleton-Century-Crofts, 1952, p. 260):

> Naturalism in literature is a moral and spiritual absolute zero, conceivable but unattainable, and the term "naturalistic," when applied to a book or an author, must be taken only in a relative sense. Perhaps Vernon L. Parrington (in *Main Currents of American Thought*, III, 323 ff.) has been clearer than any other critic when he listed the criteria of naturalism in fiction as: 1) an attempted objectivity; 2) frankness; 3) an amoral attitude toward material; 4) a philosophy of determinism; 5) pessimism; 6) the projection of "strong" characters of marked animal or neurotic nature.
>
> For all practical purposes, a book in which some of these characteristics are found to a marked degree can be classed as "naturalistic"; the purely naturalistic work has never been written and, if written, probably could never be read.

Indeed, we not infrequently hear the claim that naturalism in fiction is now dead. So, for example, Horace Victor Gregory, writing, on "Mutations of Belief in the Contemporary Novel" in the symposium *Spiritual Problems in Contemporary Literature* (ed. Stanley Romaine Hopper, Harper, 1952, p. 40):

> Between 1918 and the present moment, the fiction of naturalism has died a natural death. This does not mean that realism has completely disappeared as one of the elements of contemporary fiction, but that the extremes of techniques in realistic fiction no longer follow the rules by which Zola was so long regarded as a master.

Mr. Gregory's implied wish may be heartily agreed with, but his statement of fact is not quite accurate. The naturalistic novel will never completely disappear from the contemporary scene, for the simple reason that as long as writers of a naturalistic complexion of mind continue to write, they will write that kind of fiction. When the education, the cultural influences that engender such a frame of mind have ceased to operate, then the naturalistic novel will have been a thing of the past. When will that be?

In the meantime, the fact that Jones' *From Here to Eternity* was hailed as giving new impetus to the naturalistic novel is proof enough that the climate yet exists, at least in the United States, in which the naturalistic novelist is still assured of a considerable reading public.

And Jones' horrendously detailed study was not the last furiously blushing rose of the American naturalistic summer. A year and a half later we were offered *Corpus of Joe Bailey*, by Oakley Hall. John K. Hutchens, reviewing the novel in the April 10, 1953, New York *Herald Tribune*, indicates its character as follows:

> But, sooner or later, you get back to that basic matter of whether the people he is writing about are interesting. And, beginning with Joe Bailey, they are not. They are pathetic but always predictable, from Joe—"not really a good guy, nor was he smart enough to get anywhere"—to his friend Peter with his terrible, guilty secret, and Joe's girl Con, haunted by a family tragedy, and the assorted oafs who are his fraternity brothers at Berkeley.
>
> But when Mr. Hall has described them all and the life they lead, consisting mainly of alcohol and bedding-down, there remains a vacuum. No one is going anywhere, no one is thinking about anything much, and Mr. Hall is up against the deadly question a writer of his school is apt to face: what of it?
>
> Because, while a naturalist's details are here by the thousand, they do not in this case do anything. Except in the most negative sense, they say nothing about the society or the time to which they belong. It follows inevitably that out of *Corpus of Joe Bailey* comes no meaning, unless Mr. Hall is simply trying to suggest that there is meaning in the very meaninglessness he is at such vast pains to convey. But if that is the case, it has to be asked whether it was worth his trouble.

This identical point can and must be made on all the books of John O'Hara, up to and including his latest, *From the Terrace*. And one of the clearest and most striking examples —because the author is a far more literate and powerful writer than most in the school—is A. E. Ellis' *The Rack*.

The perdurance of the naturalistic trend in literature, the assessment of its rise and fall, of its influence here and now, is not just a simple question of hard and fast boundaries passed once for all; it is rather a question of the pendulum ceaselessly swinging. Right now, even in American letters, the swing is away from naturalism; a decade hence the impetus may be all in the other direction. We are dealing, after all, with perennial attitudes of mind rather than with mere popularities of technique. That is why it has seemed worth while to expend this rather long discussion on naturalism. Its absolute existence in literature may indeed be comparable to the absolute zero in physics, but its continuing and insidious pervasiveness in human thought must always be reckoned with if literature is to be properly criticized.

The shades and degress of naturalism found in actual practice make the critic's most difficult task that of assessing properly the realistic novel that is tinged with naturalism but not so steeped in it as to be obviously indictable. Such books are fairly well represented by Daphne du Maurier's *My Cousin Rachel*. This is a book, I believe, which is quite representative of the naturalistic threat. What might have been the moral fiber of the story is weakened because the conflict between good and evil has been reduced to the level of expediency and social acceptability. The realism is under the beginnings of the naturalistic blight; the unreality of a starker naturalism has not yet sucked from the book all the strength that comes from contact with real life and with the whole of real life.

To complicate still further the business of accurate and fair-minded criticism, there is a good percentage of books every year which seem on first impression to be naturalistic to some degree but which are not naturalistic at all. These are the novels which deal with *characters* who are largely motivated by a naturalist philosophy or approach to life, but in whose lack of values the author does not concur. I believe that John Marquand is somewhat a master of this type of fiction. Charles Gray in *Point of No Return*, Geoffrey Wilson in *So Little Time*, General Melville Goodwin in *Melville Goodwin, U.S.A.*, Willis Wayde in *Sincerely, Willis Wayde* and Thomas Harrow in *Women and Thomas Harrow* are, to be sure, no counterparts of O'Hara's Grace Tate. But they are, to some extent at least, persons whose realization of spiritual truths is dim and faltering. And yet I believe that the thoughtful reader sees that Marquand is not depicting their seminaturalistic attitudes with a note of warm approval in his voice. He rather talks about them in an undertone of oblique criticism, understanding with deep sympathy how they got to view life as they do, but suggesting at the same time that they would be much more human, much more real, if they viewed life differently—not naturalistically, but realistically.

And the real, I repeat, includes the spiritual, as Marquand, according to my reading of him, seems to hint. This quiet depth in Marquand, strangely missed by many critics, has been admirably summarized by Charles A. Brady in his essay on the novelist in *Fifty Years of the American Novel* (p. 113). He says:

> This dual power of reflecting objective reality without distortion and, at the same time, fulfilling the old Morality function of representing Everyman to himself . . . ought not to be taken lightly in an age which, instead of holding a mirror up to nature, prefers to reflect back from a monomaniac monocle its own myopic eye. With Marquand's courteously relentless assistance

94

we look at our natural face in a mirror; and then go about our various businesses. Only, instead of forgetting what kind of men we are, perhaps, for the first time, we realize what kind of men we are.

These moderating elements can all enter into the picture and demand a nicety of judgment from the critic. But naturalism, when it does show its head unabashedly, is a thing that is easily spotted. Once spotted, it is not very hard to show that it is not based on reality, despite its appearance of being but a development of realism. It has rather come round full circle and ends in being quite divorced from reality.

This is not at all a surprising result. One who, on principle, rejects part of reality might just as well reject the whole and logically ought to do so. In philosophy, the positivist who says that only what he can estimate by his senses has value, has passed a judgment whose truth is something that cannot be estimated by the senses. Therefore this very judgment is a thing of no value. He has consequently no place whereon to lay hold of reality. In excluding the highest ranges of reality, spiritual reality, from his scale of values, he has deprived himself of any scale of values. And so in literature the naturalistic writer, in denying the highest realities of human life and human nature, automatically reduces the other realities, the physical facts of life, to a meaningless jumble. They can no longer be fitted into any rational pattern.

But not all realism in literature need result in this paralysis. There is another type of realism possible, and most of the novels by leading Catholic authors which have aroused hostile criticism even from some Catholic critics during the past few years are novels which have been characterized by a realism which I believe must be called idealistic. These novels have been realistic because they have told the truth demanded by their subject matter. They have been idealistic because in telling the

95

truth they have recognized and even proclaimed the reality and the supreme importance of truths and values that transcend the world of sense. And they have done this very frequently through characters who seem to deny those truths and values.

Examine, in the light of this discussion, Graham Greene's *The End of the Affair*. Under its realism, which is indeed frank and unsparing, there is the clear and even impassioned realization that there are some supreme values at stake. In her struggles against crowding temptations and even in her frequent failures, Sarah ultimately came to face the fact that she had to make a moral decision, that it was hers alone to make and that eternal issues hinged upon it. Even when such a decision ends in apparent failure (as did Scobie's in *The Heart of the Matter*) the idealism still perdures. The decision was set before Scobie and through him before the reader. If Scobie failed, then he is in very good literary company, for so did Macbeth, and Francesca and Paolo, and the nameless little priest of Greene's *The Power and the Glory* and hundreds of others of the vivid characters of literature who indeed failed, but not until they had faced a moral issue and wrestled with it with groanings of spirit and agonies of soul. Even in their failure they still give testimony that there are realities in the world greater than the body and what it eats and wears. No naturalistic realist can ever portray characters who give such testimony. That our Catholic authors have done so is a testimony that in their realism they are idealists.

We may go a little further than this. There is in realistic literature that is at the same time idealistic a deeper and wider recognition of suprasensible reality. In addition to the specific spiritual value that is at stake in a particular book, there are other more general spiritual realities which are treated by way of implication. *Macbeth* is more than a story of temptation to murder finally yielded to. *The End of the Affair* is more than a tale of marital infidelity finally repented of. These books and others of which they are types have a lot to say about three great fundamental human virtues. They are the virtues of faith, hope and charity.

Of these three virtues perhaps hope is more susceptible to practical demonstration in broadening this portion of our discussion. First there is a caution to be issued. When we speak of the virtue of hope in this context we do not necessarily mean the theological virtue of hope. A virtue is called theological when it is exercised under the impulse of grace with God as its formal object. Some books, of course, are concerned in that way with the virtue of hope. Devotional writing, for example, may treat specifically the virtue of hope in its direct reference to God, as it may the virtues of faith and charity. This type of reading aside, however, books in general and particularly fiction will not be interested usually or necessarily in hope as a theological virtue. But literature does have a lot to say about the natural virtue of hope, which may be defined as an anticipation of good for ourselves and for others.

A little reflection will perhaps show that almost all the great literature of the world is at base concerned with this idea of hope. This follows almost automatically from the initial fact treated earlier in our discussion, that such a predominant amount of literature is concerned with the theme of conflict. In almost every great book—at least in every great book that deals with human relationships—there is always, under whatever guise, a hero and a villain. This hero and villain are locked in conflict. There is a fight going on. We have, as a matter of fact, in our common parlance the phrase "while there's life, there's hope." The Irish strain in any of us would probably prompt us to say quite cheerily, that "while there's a *fight*, there's hope." And we would not be far wrong, at that, for to fight, one has to be alive. As long as the conflict in the book continues, there is life and consequently hope. Hope for what?

97

Hope that the hero, the good, will win through; hope that the villain, the evil, will be vanquished.

This fundamental fact may be somewhat dramatized if one were able to imagine that he was seeing *Macbeth* for the first time on any stage. The trouble frequently is that now we know the stories of these classics so well that their original impact is a little lost on us. But if you were seeing the play for the first time what would be your reactions? The first reaction would be one of suspense. Will Macbeth see through the promptings of his wife? Will he shake off the spell of the weird sisters? Will he actually go through with his plan of murder and, if he does, will he repent and try somehow to undo the wrong? Until the final curtain falls the struggle goes on. Though Macbeth gets engulfed deeper and deeper, we can and do cherish the hope that this once noble character will not fall.

He *does* fall, but in the matter of engendering the hope of which we are here speaking, that ultimate failing does not matter. What we see is an acting out of the fact that failure comes only after a struggle and, in the truly great literature of the world, after a titanic struggle. We have seen an acting out of the fact that despite the weaknesses that debilitate our human nature as a legacy from original sin, human nature does not take to great evil spontaneously and thoughtlessly. Man has to be, as it were, coached into great evil and sin, and even after he has learned his part exceedingly well, he may still through his free will throw off the role and vanquish the villain. In other words, this type of literature is a constant reminder that there are sound objective reasons (and not mere sentimental wish-thinking) for seeing, even in the characters that ultimately fail, their testimony to the truth of human nature, namely that man does not choose evil without a realization, however dim, of what he is hazarding. This is testimony again that there are goals that man can reach, that human nature is in its essential make-up an aspiring nature, a nature that hopes.

In whom, precisely, does this hope reside? In the characters in the book? Or in the reader? A further analysis would probably show that it is the character's struggle, postulating in him some sense of aspiration, that engenders a similar hope in the reader. An extension of this thought would show how the values of which literature speaks, or at which it hints, can be and are carried over into life. If I have seen in my reading that hope is one of the mainsprings of human action, then I can look with a hopeful eye on human beings with whom I come in contact. It will not be any subjective sentimentality or emotionalism, but a characteristic objectively present in human beings and brought into focus in literature that will enable me to maintain that I have a rational ground for being hopeful about people—about their success in overcoming this or that particular trouble or temptation and indeed, ultimately, about their eternal destiny.

This is not, I believe, to read too much into the purpose or function of a good book, because any good book will portray human nature as it actually or really (realistically) is. And human nature as it is is frail, but at the same time majestic with the majesty that comes to it from its power to aspire, from its power to seek, across and through the allurements of the here and the now and across and through all time into eternity, the "beauty that is ever ancient and ever new." There is an even deeper majesty, of course. It is the majesty that is human nature's because it can not only seek but actually find. The aspiration can fructify to its destined term—it can reach the goal.

A wonderfully moving example of how the virtue of hope is woven into the very stuff of literature is provided by a passage in *The Man on a Donkey*, H. F. M. Prescott's monumental chronicle of the times of Henry VIII. The passage concerns one Gib Dawe, a priest who has been seduced by the "new learning" of the times, who has fallen into habitual sin and, finally, yielded to despair. He, to be sure, does not hope; he has lost the capacity to hope. Yet his very hopelessness is the ground for the reader's realization that it is man's duty and glory to hope even apparently against hope. The passage runs:

> For now he knew that though God might save every other man, Gib Dawe He could not save. Once he has seen his sin as a thing that clung close as his shadow clung to his heels; now he knew that it was the very stuff of his soul. Never could he, a leaking bucket not to be mended, retain God's saving Grace, however freely outpoured. Never could he, that heavy lump of sin, do any other than sink, and sink again, however often Christ, walking on the waves, should stretch His hand to lift and bring him safe.
>
> He did not know that though the bucket be leaky it matters not at all when it is deep in the deep sea, and the water both without it and within. He did not know, because he was too proud to know, that a man must endure to sink, and sink again, but always crying upon God, never for shame ceasing to cry, until the day when he shall find himself lifted by the bland swell of that power, inward, secret, as little to be known as to be doubted, the power of omnipotent grace in tranquil, irresistible operation.

Admittedly not every book, even those by the Catholic idealists of whom we are treating, can be fitted snugly and patly into this scheme of criticism. There are borderline cases. What can be made, for example, of Pinkie, the sinister little "hero" in Graham Greene's *Brighton Rock?* It would seem that he does not engage in much moral struggle. And yet *Brighton Rock* is a fine book if not precisely a great one. Pinkie is an adolescent gangster and murderer who slays callously and almost blissfully. But notice that he does not sin thoughtlessly. He has a clear conception that he is jeopardizing his immortal soul; he knows that he matters, that he is playing for supreme stakes. Though he seems to take no active part in any struggle against the evil that is almost ingrained in him, he is nevertheless the battleground of awe-ful forces. He does not, I admit, engender much hope, but even his extraordinary character (Greene is essaying here almost a study in abnormality) still gives testimony that hope is not beyond his reach. It is consequently not beyond our hope for him because, warped and twisted though he is, he is still a moral agent.

The protagonists in a purely naturalistic literature, on the other hand, do not provide the reader with any ground for hope either in themselves or by extension in human nature as it is met in real life. They do not provide it because a naturalist by definition cannot hope, since hope is one of those intangibles that has for him no value. If it does exist at all, it is on a lower level of social struggle, of economic survival, of expediency. Studs Lonigan, in the once shocking Farrell novels, for example, is certainly engaged in a surly conflict, but it is merely a brawl with organized society which, he whimpers, does him wrong.

The "heroes" of our naturalistic literature are actually characters who *do not matter*. It makes little difference to any experienced reader whether or not Grace Tate in John O'Hara's *A Rage to Live* or Prewitt in James Jones' *From Here to Eternity* break off their habits of sin—the reader cannot get interested in them *as persons*. But the very fact that so many readers have been concerned almost with real anxiety over the fate of Scobie in *The Heart of the Matter* and of Sarah in *The End of the Affair*—that fact of itself is proof that Graham Greene thinks that Scobie and Sarah did matter, that the reader thinks Scobie and Sarah matter, because both Greene and the reader know that human personality is a thing that matters tremendously.

There is little need to spend much time analyzing the natural virtue of faith in this particular literary connection. It goes hand in hand with the hope that we have been discussing. If a character in a story engages in the struggle which manifests the fact that he hopes, he does it because he has a certain amount of faith in himself, a certain amount of trust and self-confidence. The reader likewise will conceive a certain amount of trust in the character. He will be willing, in other words, to give the character the chance to struggle against his difficulties and temptations and win through. Idealistic realism, accordingly, is always at least by strong implication engaged in the assertion that human nature is a stuff that deserves our faith and our hope.

There is a still further implication in the works of the idealistic realists—they inevitably lay the ground for the operation of the virtue of natural charity. This indeed is the highest quality an author can infuse into his work and the richest value a receptive reader can harvest from the reading. How is charity involved in the work, for example, of the Catholic realists we have mentioned?

It is involved first because it is, as it were, imbedded in the very subject matter. The *thing* talked about, the raw material which is molded into character and situation in Mauriac, Bernanos, Greene, Waugh, Undset, Sullivan—to take some scattered examples from various national literatures—is a *thing* that is deserving of love. And what is that thing? In wide terms it is the moral law and its application, violations of it, adherence to it, in all the variations with which, in the concrete, human nature faces the fact of the existence of that law. Beyond that and on a plane essentially higher, the *thing* talked about by these Catholic realists is not merely moral law but the supernatural elevation of human nature through grace. On this plane the same variations of human reaction may be portrayed—the fact of this elevation may be but dimly realized by the characters in the story, or they may embrace it with feeble or fervent arms. But the reality of that elevation will be more or less evident, and that reality is, again, a thing deserving of love. As long as the author keeps this reality present—no matter how his characters may react to it—he has informed his subject matter with love. That is to say, the author sees as he writes that the moral world and the supernatural world are things to be loved, and as we read we are likely to catch a glimpse of the same truth. There will be more to say on this matter of literature as a source of charity when we come later to consider the meaning of the "apostolate of the pen."

Moral and supernatural values are, as a matter of fact, in themselves proper objects of love, however irksome and stringent at times may be the obligations they put upon us to prove the reality of our theoretical love by reducing it to practical action. This, I believe, is what our Catholic authors concretely portray through their characters who do not live up to the stringent and irksome demands. What else is a character like Scobie in *The Heart of the Matter* revealing on every page of the story save that, though he was largely plunged into bewilderment by the burden of these demands, he did at the same time dimly realize that they were deserving of his fidelity and love? What other motive impelled him to struggle against his temptations before he actually fell?

An atmosphere of charity, then, is at the base of idealistic realism. This point is frequently overlooked simply because of the fact that most contemporary Catholic authors are somewhat laconic about it. It is an attitude that they entertain and project perhaps unconsciously, and certainly without calling explicit attention to it. After all, it's demanding a lot from an author to ask him to say "why" he wrote a book. If one asked Kathryn Hulme why she wrote her controversial *The Nun's Story*, she would probably not say: "because I had the virtue of charity in mind"—but she would have had it in mind, for the simple reason that *love* is at the basis of all concern for others in the relationships set up in novelistic conflict. But neither authors nor characters state this concern in so many terms. As Neville Braybrooke writes ("Catholics and the Novel," *Blackfriars*, February, 1950), referring to the end of *The Heart of the Matter*:

> [This] is an example of the way in which Greene has brought to perfection a conflict without resolving the problem in terms of mortal and venial sins, but rather leaving such a judgment to the Omnipotent, his task as author being merely to present the crisis in human terms. Furthermore, it is this precise refusal to pass judgment on their characters which has caused a charge to be made in Catholic circles that novels such as that of Greene cause scandal.

And it is precisely because that particular problem is present in *human terms*, in terms of humanity as the idealist sees it, and as the naturalist cannot see it, that it will involve the realization that the elements that go to make up the problem are things in themselves lovable—values, truths, realities that are rooted in charity and constitute a motive for charity.

There is a further way in which charity enters into the total equipment of the idealistic realist. This is in his relationship to his characters, the people of his own imaginative creation. This truth may perhaps be illustrated by its opposite. Many, if not most, naturalistic authors give the impression that they have hardly more than a sniggering contempt for the children of their own artistic travail. Sinclair Lewis, for example, in the earlier days when he could write, was neither artistically nor morally at fault in the mere fact of drawing the portraits of his Babbitts and Gantrys. He *was* artistically (and perhaps even morally) at fault in his own attitude toward them. I believe that attitude can aptly be summed up by saying, as I wrote of *Kingsblood Royal*, that one had the impression while reading it that one was "not sharing an experience but watching an experiment." If that is true, it is a prostitution of the whole process of artistic creation. After all, the only reason why the human artist can (as we inaccurately term the process) "create" anything lies fundamentally in the fact that he himself was, as we accurately say, created. The artist's ability to "make" is but a dim reflection and imitation of God's creative power. Now, God does not create anything for the purpose of hating or despising it or being indifferent to it. Insofar as the artist makes anything for the purpose of turning it into the object of his bitterness or contempt or indifference, he is negating the very act of creation in which he is engaging.

This strange coldness toward the characters in their own stories can be discovered in all the writers of the naturalistic school. It is a blight that has plagued Lewis, Farrell, O'Hara, Caldwell and others among our American practitioners; it is a blight that but recently infected the proponents of existentialism. It is the blight that has never touched those who are deeply humanist, much less those motivated by the idealism of which we are here speaking. This is not to say that the naturalist writer is not *interested* in his characters. He is, else he would never have begun to write about them. But his interest so often strikes one as a mere clinical inquisitiveness, a detached examination of the specimen under the microscope. Specimens so examined are generally dead.

It is, of course, true that sympathy for his characters may bog the author down in sentimentality, in an excessive emotionalism, but there is a middle ground, a balance between the cynicism of the naturalist and the sentimentality of the emotionalist; this is the middle ground to which the Catholic realist by and large adheres. The marital vagaries of Julia in *Brideshead Revisited*, of Sarah in *The End of the Affair*, the self-deception about her own charitableness of Brigitte Pian in Mauriac's *Woman of the Pharisees*, are not treated with any sentimental dilution of "Oh, the poor things just could not help themselves, you see." Neither, on the other hand, are those characters despised or belittled in the ruthless probing of their hidden motives. They are, in the true sense of the word, appreciated. That means that they are seen for what they are. And what they are are human beings who may be weak and variable, stubborn in their attachment to evil or quick to shake it off, but still possessed of that dignity that crowns them by the fact that they are human beings—in other words, by the fact that they are objects, worthy, at least potentially, of love.

In these two large fashions, then, if in no others, the Catholic realist deals with the stuff of charity. This admirable traffic, to be sure, is not the sole exercise of Catholic novelists. It is part of the equipment of any realist who does not exclude human (moral and spiritual) ideals from the ambit of his view of life. We have but to recall such authors as Willa Cather in all her works, Alan Paton in *Cry, the Beloved Country*, John Hersey in *The Wall*, Herman Wouk in *The Caine Mutiny*, Anne Fremantle in *James and Joan*, Helen Waddell in *Peter Abelard*, Henrietta Buckmaster in *Bread from Heaven*, H. F. M. Prescott in *The Man on a Donkey* and dozens of others, to realize how charity (most critics are wedded to the word "compassion," perhaps because it sounds less religious) is woven into the very fabric of literature that is truly human.

By way of underscoring this discussion of realism as generally practiced by Catholic novelists, I would like to include a reference to an article I wrote in the December 17, 1955, issue of *America*. The article dealt with two valuable documents, both of which treated the opportunities and the responsibilities of the Catholic author in writing realistically of the world around him. They admirably reinforce my stand that "realism" is not, of itself, something that a Catholic novelist has to flee as though it necessarily implied a naturalistic, sex-obsessed approach to authorship.

The two documents were, first, an article that appeared in

the January, 1955, issue of *Criterio* (Buenos Aires), by Msgr. Gustave J. Franceschi, editor of the Catholic biweekly, and second, a pastoral letter issued by the German hierarchy, dated October 21, 1955. The full text of the German pastoral (the most weighty of the two documents) will be found in the February, 1956, issue of the *Catholic Mind*. On these two statements I commented as follows:

> The pastoral rejoices that Catholic novelists are concerned "with questions that arise from religion." We must be grateful, the bishops say, "that they paint no wishful picture of human existence, its struggles, defeats and triumphs—no sentimentalized . . . and therefore untrue picture—but that they are concerned to mirror reality."
>
> The reality mirrored is often dark. The German bishops realize this and do not rebuke the novelists for reflecting the world as it is. "We do not fail to see," they state, "that to call things by their right names, and to recognize the power of the evil in the world, is of great value not merely for literature but also for the pastoral duties of our times. This kind of literature gives rise to shocks which can have a wholesome effect."
>
> It is at this point that the article in *Criterio* reinforces the stand of the German bishops. Under the title "Las Necesidades Espirituales de Hoy" (Today's Spiritual Needs), Monsignor Franceschi discusses the effect that novels such as those by Graham Greene and François Mauriac have or should have on the intelligent reader. The author's conclusion is that "these books that disquiet our passivity and show that so many of us do not really know the world in which we live" are "useful" works, just as the "*Confessions* of St. Augustine were when they were written."
>
> The reason why such works disturb some readers, says Monsignor Franceschi, is that they do not realize the "effect that the milieu, the doctrines of the day, customs and the political and economic regime exercise on souls." Nor have they realized in concrete instances the different temptations that rise for "the

young person living tranquilly at home and the other who has to
get himself daily to work to earn his keep."

To realize—to make real to one's self—that is the problem.
And yet, there is still another problem. How can the author make
us, the readers, realize the evil in today's world without settling
for a mere diagnosis? This is what the German bishops turn their
main attention to in their pastoral. "To sum up," they say,

We find that a large section of our Catholic literature prefers
the darker sides of life. In that it is in accord with the literature
of our times, and no doubt valuable if it desires to set a whole-
some diagnosis of our time against euphemistic descriptions.
We would go so far as to speak of the duty of giving such a
diagnosis; and there is no need for our writers to feel that
their freedom is limited by bourgeois prejudices. But . . . it
would also be desirable if, beyond a mere diagnosis, man in
his needs could be helped by literature; if he were saved from
the false, fateful impression that there is an unbridgeable gulf
between the sober reality of life and the moral law as this is
given by God and proclaimed by the Church. We do not speak
for a literature of false pieties, but we do speak for a literature
which, in addition to making a diagnosis of our times, con-
tributes to their cure.

Perhaps the most practical counsel the German bishops give is
contained at the end of the pastoral. Far from condemning the
works of the Catholic realists, they simply and sanely say:

So far as our faithful are concerned, we should like to urge
them to discriminate in the choice of reading matter. . . . They
should remember that not every book is suitable to everyone.
. . . Our Catholic librarians and their helpers should be mind-
ful of the characteristics of works addressed to readers who are
mature and firm in their moral and religious outlook, so that
their libraries, the use of which we strongly recommend, should
indeed harm no one, but offer each his own fare.

Finally, the bishops say, and here they come into closer accord
with the *Criterio* article:

108

Thanks are due to our Catholic writers for their work in the service of the word that ultimately points to God. We feel ourselves through our own divine mission united with them and ask their help in the present tasks of the Church.

One of the tasks of the Church, says the *Criterio* article, is performed by Catholic novelists whose works "sound like an alarm-bell to the ears of those who think that they are living in a world substantially Christian."

This brief summary does justice neither to the pastoral of the German bishops nor to the article in *Criterio*. They must both be read in full. But that so much space and thought have been devoted to the role of the Catholic novelist is at once a tribute to the work that has been done and an acknowledgment that creative fiction is a magnificent tool for the dissemination of the word "that ultimately points to God."

The burden of these thoughts may indeed have seemed to limit the discussion to a provincially partisan treatment of Catholic authors. That is because my aim has been to show that the charge of realism leveled against our contemporary Catholic novelists by no means marks them with a stigma. There is realism *and* realism, it must be remembered, and the kind that ponders, perhaps unobtrusively and only by implication, the truth that human nature and the ideals that can motivate it are hope-inspiring and love-generating, is a realism that is sane and Christian.

A provocative statement by Mr. Braybrooke in the *Blackfriars* article mentioned above perhaps sums this up best. He writes: "Novel writing is essentially, when seen in a broad perspective, a quest whose aim is to come face to face with Him in whose image all men are made. Properly understood in this context, there can be no such thing as secular literature."

It is impossible to discover such a reflection in naturalistic writers. It may be difficult to trace its neat application in some sane realists. It is fairly easy to see the truth of it shining through the work of contemporary Catholic realists.

This idea of the challenge literature offers to the exercise of at least a natural charity will come up again for further discussion when I take up in Part III the shortcomings of viewing literature merely as a means to mutual understanding.

PART III
PRINCIPLES ON THE
FUNCTION OF LITERATURE

Principles on the Function of Literature

LET US now go on to examine at greater length the role of literature as teacher, while at the same time keeping in mind the last of the five principles we have discussed above in Part I— namely, that literature, though its primary and formal purpose is not to act as schoolmaster, does nevertheless impart a certain amount of instruction or knowledge or wisdom to its readers.

If literature be this kind of a teacher, instructing informally and subordinately to the purpose of imparting legitimate pleasure, it would be logical to suppose that some principles exist which give direction to its instructional aspects. These principles are literary; they are not moral or pedagogical in the sense of being derived from the study of morals or pedagogy as such. They are derived rather from a consideration of what art is, of what literature is. They are in part *a priori*, drawn from an abstract consideration of what the aims of artistic creation are; and in part *a posteriori*, drawn from a consideration of actual works of art, of how the artifact bears out the theory. They are principles, indeed, for all literature, but they have special relevance for Catholic writers and readers.

The suggestion to examine these principles was occasioned by an article in the *Saturday Review of Literature* for September 7, 1946. There the Canadian novelist, Hugh MacLennan, discussed the place of the newly important Canadian literature in relation to the whole literary tradition of Western civilization. The particular Canadian application is not here our immediate concern; it was Mr. MacLennan's statement about literary tradition in the Western world which started the wheels of thought whirling. The mainstream of that tradition, he contends, was "the cycle which had its origins in the Renaissance." This culture, he continues,

> was truly international. In spite of national boundary lines, the writing of Germany, France, England and the smaller nations of Europe has in the main mirrored a society which for century after century held more or less common philosophies and more or less common points of view.

Unfortunately, Mr. MacLennan feels, this culture has run its day. He goes on:

> The society which produced Shakespeare and Racine has reached a point at which Celine and Dali [are] considered to be, not freaks, but interpreters of the life around them. . . . It is the final, dying gasps of the Renaissance culture which have been heard in Europe during the last decades. . . .

The upshot is, he pleads, that North American culture, already "split wide apart from Europe," should begin to produce writers and critics who will no longer "look to Europe as a model," who will cease imitating the "decadent spirit of the great masters of the European decline."

It is, of course, possible to disagree with this analysis on the perfectly valid ground that Western cultural and literary tradition springs from roots older and deeper than those planted during the Renaissance. This, however, is not the exact point here. The point is that whenever the roots of this Western tradition may have been planted, the fruit of it still continues to burgeon. That tradition has not died out. It still exists and is still potent. Indeed, its force and vigor are now growing. This growth is to be seen particularly in Catholic letters, since it is particularly here that there is discernible a common body of principles, a common approach to authorship, criticism and reading.

1 . Literature as a Moral Activity

THE SOURCE of this common body of principles so far predates the Renaissance that we are forced back to Aristotle to discover it. Just as Cardinal Newman in a famous passage once claimed that thinking man in the West will always be an Aristotelian, so it may be said that all Catholic literary people, whether creators or enjoyers, take their stand, albeit at times unwittingly, with Aristotle. Now, it is a prime concept in Aristotle's thought about the function of literature that this aspect of man's intellectual activity is a serious business. Poetry, he says (and here I borrow from the essay, "Catholicism and English Literature," in *Essays in Reconstruction*, edited by Dom Ralph Russell, O.S.B., Sheed & Ward, 1946, p. 80):

> "imitates" nature, not indeed by slavishly copying it but by dividing the end toward which nature is working in some particular instance and by realizing or illustrating that operation in another medium. Art, then, deals with the very stuff of life, takes up some incident from it, and makes explicit the end and the principles inherent in that incident by excluding the uncertainty and incompleteness which envelope it in real life. *We are shown rather what men "ought" to be than what they actually are* [my emphasis].

This "oughtness" has to be properly understood. I have remarked above that an author sets out in his story simply to tell us how his characters actually did act in a particular set of circumstances; he does not preach about those characters or actions. He must do this by "imitating" the actions as he conceives them actually to have happened, or as they did in reality happen, if he is writing a strictly historical novel. Since the actions he is thus imitating were both good and bad actions—and the whole gamut in between—these actions will find place in his picturing of the characters and situation. But the poet, Aristotle's thought implies, is not a "historian dealing with actual events and bound by particular facts"—and this is also true of the creative novelist insofar as he is creative. "Neither is he a philosopher who uses concrete particulars as a starting point for his primary business of abstraction. The poet [read novelist] is concerned rather with the general or idealized truth inseparable from concrete human action." (I take these explanations of Aristotle's thought from an admirable essay on *The Poetics*, by Francis X. Connolly, in *The Great Books: A Christian Appraisal*, vol. II, Devin-Adair, 1950, p. 36.)

It is this "general, idealized truth," lurking, as it were, beneath and behind the concrete actions and situations in a novel, that will constitute the "oughtness" that is implicit in the act of imitation which is the essence of artistic creation. This view is by no means a plea for literature to mount the pulpit and start moralizing. Indeed, if we were to demand that of Aristotle, we would be parting company with him at the very outset. He repudiated poetry's being "held responsible for the explicit performance of a moral office," since its object is "the contemplative pleasure of imitation and not the direct imitation of abstract truth" (to quote Dr. Connolly once again). Hence it is that "the good moral effect of poetry [literature] can come only by indirect means."

It may be obvious here how we are thrown back on the remarks made in Part I on the doctrine of the "esthetic distance," which is in truth but an immediate application of the Aristotelian creed on "imitation."

This Aristotelian concept is still, in the main, the concept that dominates Catholic writing and ought to dominate Catholic criticism and reading. The fact that it *is* held, though perhaps implicitly and unconsciously, is revealed by a sort of congenital uneasiness among Catholic readers over the photographic and reportorial type of writing that bulked so large in the American fiction of the twenties and thirties and which still crops up today. The Catholic who has read books like Steinbeck's *The Wayward Bus* or Jones' *From Here to Eternity*, though he is in all honesty impelled to admit that the slices of life have been caught vividly and can be verified in actual experience all around him, still feels a vague suspicion that this kind of book somehow *cannot* really be called literature. What this reader is unconsciously saying to himself is that these books have fallen short of the Aristotelian concept of what art is or ought to be.

Such books have photographed a montage of contemporary life; their clicking of the shutter has often been marvelously timely and vivid. But they have merely caught men acting as they do and not rather as they "ought." In these books and others like them there is no clear perception of ultimate ends and purposes. A frozen moment of social or marital life, let us say, is caught in the story, but the problems and acts of *this* particular social group receive no illumination from any clear vision of the goals and purposes of social life in itself; *this* particular marriage is not illuminated by any light flowing from a clear realization of the intrinsic ends and purposes of the very institution of marriage.

This is why, in Aristotle's concept, art is essentially, if indirectly, a moral activity—the individual act captured in the creative activity always implies a relationship toward ends and purposes. Such a relationship is a moral fact, and the portrayal of such relationship is a moral activity. It is in this sense that art is always, at least implicitly, didactic, for if "man learns first by imitation," says Aristotle, and if it is "natural for all to delight in works of imitation," it is further true that "to be learning something is the greatest of pleasures not only for the philosophers but also for the rest of mankind, however small their capacity for it; the reason for the delight in seeing the picture is that one is at the same time learning." Think back, here, if I may suggest it, to the earlier remarks on the *rational* pleasure which is literature's first purpose.

Perhaps an illustration may be taken from portraiture. It will be admitted, I suppose, that photography is not, strictly speaking, an art. It *must* be admitted if you are an Aristotelian. For the photograph, catching the subject in the split second of the shutter's release, immobilizes the human features, just, and only, as they instantaneously are. The portrait painter, on the other hand, working over days and weeks, will complete a human face which at no time during the sittings looked exactly and completely as it does in the finished product. It will, however, and marvelously enough, by having caught the varying shades of mood, temperament and personality that played over the features during the sittings, be a truer picture because of its composite growth. The painter will have reproduced the human face as it "ought" to be to reflect this particular personality; the photographer will have merely caught the human countenance as it actually *was* merely at a particular point of time.

This moral approach to the function of art is admittedly a narrow gate and a strait path. If interpreted in a doctrinaire and apologetic way it leads directly into preachment through art. This was all too evident some two decades ago in the Marxist line that was to be clearly traced in some fairly mature fiction. Such an approach may lead to Catholic preachment as well, if one forgets that the morality—the "oughtness"—of the Aristotelian concept is an inherent relationship of the reality with the ideal and not an overt elaboration of the ideal superimposed upon the reality.

This concept of literature's function was once current coin in the language of critics. One has only to browse through Coleridge, Hazlitt, De Quincey, to see that they were nurtured in this tradition. It continues through Eliot, through Maritain, and it was given rather striking expression by Van Wyck Brooks in his *On Literature Today* (Dutton, 1941, pp. 11–12), in which he called Chekhov to testify to the same perennial phenomenon:

> You may agree [says Mr. Brooks] with a further observation which I have found in Chekhov's letters: "Let me remind you that the writers who, we say, are for all time, or are simply good, or who intoxicate us, have one common and very important characteristic. They are going toward something and they are summoning you toward it, too, and you feel not with your mind, but with your whole being, that they have some object . . . The best of them are realists and paint life as it is, but, through every line's being soaked in the consciousness of an object, you feel, besides life as it is, the life which ought to be, and that captivates you."

I do not know, and perhaps Mr. Brooks does not either, whether Chekhov ever read Aristotle, but certainly there could be no more startling agreement than this between the Russian artist and the Greek philosopher.

More, Chekhov goes on to make a humble confession which certainly applies less to him than to many in the too long popular American naturalistic tradition. Says the Russian: "We paint life as it is, but beyond that—nothing at all. We have neither immediate nor remote aims, and in our soul there is a great empty space."

Mr. Brooks then goes on to descant on Chekhov's theme. He boasts that "we have writers who do not convey this impression [of the empty spaces in the soul], writers who make us feel what ought to be and for whom life is noble and important. In [these writers] one feels a joyous confidence in human nature, an abounding faith in the will, a sense of the heroic in the human adventure, good will, the leaven of existence."

He then recalls a remark of John Butler Yeats, the father of the famous Irish poet. Yeats quoted an old friend who had been for fifty years on the bench in Dublin, hearing criminal cases. When asked what had most impressed him in his half-century of hearing such human tragedies, the old judge said: "The goodness of human nature." Mr. Brooks goes on (p. 13):

> I have never forgotten this remark, and I have always felt that literature, if it is to carry out its function, must contain this germ of faith, and that the greatest literature has always done so . . . The mood of health, will, courage, faith in human nature, is the dominant mood in the history of literature. It is the warp of literature—the rest is the woof.

I ought really apologize for dwelling on this facet of our discussion here, as it will come up again when we get into the discussion of "literature as inspiration." But the two aspects —of the indirectly moral function of literature and the concrete expression of this function through the mode of aspiration, of hope, of faith—are so obviously recalls to the Aristotelian doctrine of the "imitative" function of literature, that I cannot refrain from pointing out how the traditions of literature in the West, so far from having been utterly sundered from their source, are seeking that source more and more in the writings of the more serious contemporary critics. If they were known and sought by readers, too, the critics' task would be eased. This basically Aristotelian concept is still operative, and it is by no means confined to Catholic novelists and critics. It is the leaven working away in almost any literature which is not purely naturalistic.

It is lamentable, therefore, to find viewers of the current literary scene announcing so flatly that the literary tradition of the Western world is cold and stiff in the morgue. A Proust, a Joyce, if you like, or a Sinclair Lewis or a James Jones, may be uttering the "dying gasps of European culture," but I cannot see that a Greene or a Waugh or a Bernanos is. The society these Catholic writers are portraying may indeed be "decadent" (as reviewers are so fond of saying without telling us just what they mean), but the cardinal point is that the authors' approach to that society, their proposing to that society of the fundamental purposes and ideals of life, are *not* decadent. In other words, to go back to the ideals of Aristotle, such authors show us their sophisticated, unpleasant, weary and blasé gallery of characters as indeed they are, but against an unmistakable background of implications of what they "ought" to be. There are no such "oughts" in Farrell, Lewis, Jones and the like.

Not all critics, indeed, fail to realize that this great Western literary tradition, being as it is but part of the *philosophia perennis*, is a still enduring thing. R. Ellis Roberts, for example, in reviewing Cyril Connolly's *The Condemned Playground* (*Saturday Review of Literature*, July 13, 1946) and remarking that Connolly must be presumed to know Eliot, Mauriac, Dubos, Bernanos, Baring, Belloc and many others writing in the Christian tradition, goes on to say: "Yet [Connolly] makes no effort in writing of the past or of the present, to estimate the part played by Christianity and the Catholic revival. Here he remains, indeed, an insular Victorian." This lack of sympathy, Mr. Roberts continues, is all the more odd since Connolly "sees so clearly the vice in modern art . . . it is the exaltation of self-expression over communication . . . nothing can effectively deal with 'elephantiasis of the ego'" save religion, which means that "purely humanist and psychological values must be superseded by spiritual and mystical values."

This, then, is the common critical approach—common to the literary traditions of historical Christendom, and common across the international boundaries of today, wherever worthy Catholic craftsmen are working. A voice identical in twofold wise speaks through all real Catholic literature. It is identical in its statement of theological and philosophical principles. It is no less identical in its reiteration of literary and critical principles.

Perhaps this stage of our discussion can be illustrated best by giving the stand of a modern Catholic author who is strategically one who can be quoted to greatest effect. The charge most likely to be raised in a discussion of literature from Aristotle's viewpoint of its morality is the charge that literature is *ipso facto* being burdened with an undue concern with religion or being viewed from a specifically ecclesiastical point of view. Mr. Waugh, the author to be immediately quoted, is of all Catholic authors now writing, very probably the one least liable to the charge of "religiosity," what with his background of sophisticated satire and aristocratic aloofness. Actually this whole discussion has nothing to do with any ecclesiastical viewpoint. It is not an *ex cathedra* definition of what Rome thinks about modern literature. Our discussion is simply a mulling over of what a great thinker once thought, a great thinker whose thought has been incorporated into the thinking of the whole civilized Western world. It is, as a matter of fact, only since the rise of the modern ultrarealistic school of fiction that that thought has been seriously challenged in its application to literature.

Now for Mr. Waugh's quotation. Writing in *Life* for April 8, 1946, in response to the question of an American admirer, as to when we might expect another *Brideshead Revisited*, Mr. Waugh has this to say:

Never. I can never hope to engage your attention again in quite the same way. I have already shaken off one of the American critics, Mr. Edmund Wilson, who once professed a generous interest in me. He was outraged (quite legitimately by his standards) at finding God introduced into my story. I believe that you can only leave God out by making your characters pure abstraction. Countless admirable writers, perhaps some of the best in the world, succeed in this. Henry James was the last of them.

The failure of modern novelists since and including James Joyce is one of presumption and exorbitance. They are not content with the artificial figures which hitherto passed so gracefully for men and women. They try to represent the whole human mind and soul and yet omit its determining character—that of being God's creature with a defined purpose.

So in my future books there will be two things to make them unpopular; a preoccupation with style and the attempt to represent man more fully, which, to me, means only one thing—man in his relation to God.

This, it strikes me, is a modern statement of the age-old concept in the West of what literature is all about. It is basically Aristotle's concept of the moral function of all art, but it goes deeper, just as the whole tenor of Aristotle's thought was crowned with greater perfection through its incorporation into the Christian synthesis. The depth consists in this: the teleology of literature, its intrinsic bent, is now to be conceived not merely as a moral matter, but as being based ultimately on the only thing that can give stability to morality—religion.

2. Literature as Fundamentally Religious

THE CONCLUSION at the end of the last chapter is undoubtedly one that seems at first sight simply untenable. If all real literature is in this Aristotelian sense moral, and if the moral accent of literature has now, because of the influence of Western Christian civilization, been deepened into a religious tone, it would seem to follow that all literature is in a sense a religious literature. That is the problem—can this be true?

I believe that there is no doubt in the world that the towering peaks of literature do break through the clouds into a world of religious values. The giants like Dante and Shakespeare, Milton and Racine, are all religious writers, since the incidents, the scenes they portray for us are consistently illuminated by the light of eternal truths that were part and parcel of these men's background and environment. Even this statement, of course, will be controverted by many who think it silly or inept to try to find any such values in mere works of the imagination. However that may be, the problem becomes even more complex when we try to apply the adjective "religious" to the vast mass of great and good, but admittedly not supreme literature. Can, for instance, such a book as *Huckleberry Finn* be called a religious work in any fair sense of the word? Perhaps the mere positing of the question will cause a smile among many.

But there is a true sense in which such a classic can legitimately be called religious. It was Hilaire Belloc, I believe, who once made a remark which sheds some light on the problem. He observed that after a lifetime of reading he had come to the mature conclusion that all the worthwhile books he had ever read were really all one book—and its title was "On a Unknown Country." Every book, he now recalled, dealt somehow or other with man's destiny, his yearnings, their frustrations, their partial fulfillments—in a word, every book was talking about that happiness, that beatitude for which Christian ethics and revelation teach us that man was made, and whose teaching is reinforced by the experiences of daily living. This happiness and beatitude is indeed to be sought in its proper degree here on earth and this is one "unknown country" that many are seeking. But to the Christian and Catholic, the true unknown country is the happiness and beatitude that will find fulfillment only in eternity.

To some that ultimate unknown country is truly quite unknown. The very existence of it comes to them as a rumor vague and distant, but still clear enough to start the divine unrest working. To others of us who have been given a clear and beautiful picture and promise of the far country, it is known more clearly and lovingly, for its Lord has not only told us of its mansions and invited us there as His brothers, but He has left us a map with every turning on the road set forth clearly, so that we may hurry on to enter its boundaries.

But for all, the ultimate country that beckons us is to some degree unknown—"eye hath not seen nor ear heard"—and literature is one way in which men seek to catch a clearer glimpse of its beauty. In this sense—and it is not too wide a sense—even a *Huckleberry Finn* is a religious work. It is a boy's search in a boy's terms, and in an American boy's terms, for what he conceives to be happiness. That his conceptions of it are hazy and funny and sometimes adolescently foolish only adds to the poignancy of our realization that just as Huck in real life would doubtless have outgrown his adolescent dreams of happiness, so we also have almost daily to grow out of incomplete conceptions of it into an ever more mature realization of what that happiness really is.

In more abstract and scholarly form, this intrinsic relationship between literature and religion has been finely discussed by the English critic, D. S. Savage, in his preface to *The Withered Branch: Six Studies in the Modern Novel* (Pellegrini and Cudahy, 1952, p. 14). Discussing the relationship between art and life, he remarks:

> While the novelist may well be devoid of the capacity for systematic abstract thought, there is no good novel which does not demonstrate, in a highly concrete and complex state, a process of thought. The common factor between the thinker and the novelist is precisely their orientation to truth . . . [But] before a novelist can embody meaning in his work, he must have discovered the pattern of meaning in existence. At its highest and most complete, his artistic task is secondary to and dependent upon a prior personal devotion to truth.

It is precisely from this relationship of art to truth, Mr. Savage goes on, that the quality of greatness enters into the concrete work of art:

> From this arises the permanence of great art and the perishability of the inferior work. Art draws its *autotelic* quality from its relation to the eternal. Great art is a vision of eternity, and the lesson it teaches is that life, in so far as it, too, embodies truth, is itself autotelic.

But from this there follows a conclusion which is the subject matter of our discussion here. Mr. Savage makes the conclusion as follows: "Orientation to truth is essentially a religious act. It implies an act of faith in the truth and a constancy of devotion to it." It may be, the English critic admits, that since we are living today "in a condition of comparative cultural disintegration, truth ceases to be represented in this unified and unifying way. This means that not only is the self-questioning modern man deprived of the inwardly and outwardly sustaining power of an established symbol of truth, but he lives in a world of manners similarly deprived of accepted significant patterns."

This fact, however, does not mean, according to Mr. Savage, that all modern literature, all modern fiction, is immediately divorced from an implicitly religious function,

> because the life of western man stands inescapably in a relation-ship to the Christian faith which has provided the foundation for his culture and his civilization, so his art is, willy-nilly, positively or negatively, in a similar position. The disintegration in which the modern novelist lives and moves is that of a *Christian* culture; what meaning it has is, inevitably, a religious meaning (p. 15).

This basic religious characteristic of literature can quite obviously be stamped on a book in many ways. Until quite modern times, however, it was a thing discernible almost at first glance. A novel almost infallibly had its heroes and its villains. There was always a clear struggle and conflict between good and evil. This phraseology sounds, I admit, rather as though all books were cast in the moralistic black and white of *East Lynn;* but I do not mean this description of how a basic religious atmosphere permeated literature to imply any such melodramatic quality. Moral issues, however, were squarely posed and if a Becky Sharp is a memorable character it is not merely because she is brilliantly portrayed as a vicious person, but because her evil is delineated against a background of characters and environment whose moral rightness silently criticizes her deformity.

In recent times, however, and particularly from the twenties, a trend set in among novelists to write books in which there were no discernible villains and heroes. In not a few of these novels one gets the inescapable impression that all the characters are villains, and what struggle goes on among them is an inarticulate and blind moiling and toiling in which society at large turns out to be the only real villain. What is at stake in such struggle is not any religious or moral or truly human value, but merely survival.

Now it is quite true that great books can be written and have been written in which practically the whole gallery of characters has been predominantly vicious or without principle, and whose creation was undertaken by the author with the precise purpose of giving, as by an accumulation of horrible examples, a picture of the sickness of society at a given time. This is the function, for example, of that mordant type of satire of which a fine example is Evelyn Waugh's *The Loved One*. This can be the legitimate function in other fields of art as well, as can be seen in Hogarth's savage criticism in his paintings of eighteenth-century English society, with its Bedlams and corruption in high places. But in all such art—verbal or pictorial —the silent chorus is ceaselessly voicing its comment: "The truth is not here, it is elsewhere; let this picture send you elsewhere to seek it."

The strange fruit of the naturalistic fiction of this century is what we may call the "uncommitted" novel. In this type of work the author, standing aloof from any even implicit act of judgment, assembles his amoral characters and dissects and analyzes and psychoanalyzes them, not for the purpose of illuminating any moral principles they violate, not with any suggestion or hint of moral indignation at their lapses and at the culture which occasions or causes these lapses, but simply because the author thinks that the characters are interesting case histories in themselves. It is true, of course, that many readers who still think, perhaps unconsciously, in terms of Western literary tradition, will get the impression that such books as Sinclair Lewis' *Cass Timberlane*, or James Gould Cozzens' *By Love Possessed* are indeed frightening pictures of modern unChristian marriage and so will read *their own* commentary into the stories. But the point is that neither author gives *in his own treatment* even a hint that he was in the least interested in the moral and basically religious problems. Our unconscious fealty to a literary tradition may impel us to try to judge such novels as obliquely achieving the moral function of literature, but the books themselves are a clean break with that very tradition. Since they are such a clean break, Mr. Savage would logically conclude—and we would be forced to concur—that they really have no "meaning."

3. *Literature as Inspiration*

I REPEAT my dominant theme, that the Western literary tradition still exists and still exercises the influence from which naturalism was such a clean break. Catholic literature is homogeneous, not only in still holding to the moral function of literature but also in taking the further logical step and basing that morality on religion. One has simply to run through the roster of Catholic literary names now prominent to mark how all of them who are writing truly fine books deal, in Waugh's phrase, with "man in his relation to God." Such books are fundamentally, if not explicitly, religious—not dogmatically, not apologetically, not preachily, but religious because concerned with the basis for the morality of human acts. Another way of saying this might be by comparing a good book not so much to the stone that is dropped into the pond as to the widening ripples that follow the impact. A book like *Woman of the Pharisees* or *The End of the Affair* does much more actually than merely report correlated incidents, or reproduce a scene or an age (this is the dropping of the stone); it further sets in motion a whole series of moral or fundamentally religious reactions both among the characters portrayed and in the reader (these are the widening ripples). This, again, is not because the author is preaching, but simply because this is the nature of literature on the one hand, and of the reader on the other.

A further way of coming to this same conclusion, it seems, is to apply to literature a distinction taken over from philosophy. That is the distinction between *finis operis* and *finis operantis*. The purpose the doer of the act has in mind (*finis operantis*) in writing a specific book may be just to tell a good story, or it may be, in addition, to reveal and thereby to some extent rectify a social ill. But beyond what he intends or even vaguely envisions, there will inevitably be an intrinsic finality, a goal inherent in the work itself (*finis operis*), and this will be operative whether the author thinks of it or intends it or not. So a gourmand may eat his food only because he likes it, but it will, nevertheless, still perform its connatural function of nourishing him. He may indeed live to eat, but he will still live because he eats. Parenthetically, it may be remarked here that many an author is guilty on this score in the matter of suggestiveness in his writing—the vivid scene, the alluring passage, may have been written with all the good intentions in the world, but its intrinsic bent, what it will quite naturally and normally occasion in the mind and soul of the normal reader, is the further result that the author may not have intended but for which he is nevertheless to some extent responsible.

There is, then, a certain purposiveness inherent in art and particularly in literature. It is there quite independently of the artist's intentions. It is there because literature, treating of the actions of men who are good or bad, is necessarily concerned with the moral atmosphere. And that atmosphere is, as we have seen, at base religious—at least in the wide and inclusive sense of enveloping man in his relationship to God.

If all this be true, we have finally worked down to the reason why, for those who write and criticize in accord with the traditions of Western culture, there can be no such thing as "art for art's sake." A short discussion of this much bandied phrase may serve to bring out a little more clearly the nature of this inherently religious function of literature.

It is quite true that the "rules" of literature are not the rules of morality. Nor are the rules of morality the rules of literature. In this sense art and morality are distinct, and art has its own autonomous standards. So, for that matter, have other human activities. There are, I suppose, certain rules for being a good runner, but a man may be a thief or a murderer and still hold world records on the track. In other words, the rules for achieving swiftness of foot are not of themselves rules which will govern moral integrity. But the rules for speed of foot are nevertheless not wholly divorced from the standards of morality. They are subordinate to norms of good living in two ways: first of all positively, insofar as all human activity is subject to the primacy of morality (and hence the runner, for example, must have a morally sound motive for running); and second, negatively, insofar as good living will check excesses that might interfere with speed of foot. A man may indeed be a thief and a Mercury. The wings on his heels will molt if he becomes a drunkard or a glutton.

Accordingly, though literature has its own autonomous norms and standards and is in that sense not extrinsically determined by the norms of morality, it is not for that reason independent of morality. It is subordinate, first of all positively, since the writer himself in the very act of writing is under the imperative of the moral "ought"—he must write for worthy ends and purposes. It is subordinate, secondly, because morality is a negative or "check" norm which will forestall excessive vulgarity, lack of restraint and other unhealthy trends, which are, even under the autonomy of literature's norms, artistic defects.

By way of an extended aside, I would like to call attention here to one of the finest discussions I know of on the "problem" of the relationship of art and morality. It is contained in *Théorie des Belles-Lettres*, by L. Longhaye, S.J. (Paris: Téqui, 1900, sixth edition). The whole of Chapter 4 (pp. 68–97) is devoted to this discussion. I would like here to call attention to some of the eminent critic's more pertinent conclusions.

He lays down the fundamental principle, which surely must

be the ground on which any critic nurtured in the whole Western cultural tradition will take his stand, that in the hypothesis that a conflict does arise between art and morality, there is only one decision that must be made. In my inadequate translation, Fr. Longhaye's thought runs as follows:

> Let us not imagine between art and morality some sort of concordat or compromise based on mutual concessions. Diplomacy has no role here—morality is either queen or nothing. Morality is the essential law which intervenes only to command, and not to obey or to treat on equal terms with human liberty. One can conceive it only as imposing itself as a rule, that is, as a superior norm that governs and judges all. Morality is the immediate reflection of the final end [the author has in mind the *causa finalis*, as scholastic philosophy would put it, which is precisely the intrinsic moral and religious bent of literature under our examination here] and just as that end dominates and measures everything, so should morality.

> Suppose we admit the contrary—suppose morality must yield before the demands of art or enter into compromise with those demands. Then it would be necessary to admit that art's end and purpose is equal or superior to morality's end and purpose, that is, to the supreme end of man and every creature. This is but to say that art is simply a means—as such, it depends on the final end, on the essential order; it is forever subordinate to that order.

If such a conflict should arise, then Fr. Longhaye has but one answer: "Perish all the beauties of the literary world! Perish all the art it would be necessary to purchase by a sacrifice of honor or decency!"

But this critic refuses to entertain the hypothesis that there *can* be a conflict between art and morality. He bases this on the implied statement that "what is harmful for the soul cannot be in itself beautiful or the source of true beauty." To establish this point, he makes the crucial distinction (so often forgotten

133

these days, both in creation and in criticism) between the striking, the sensational, the mere "effect," and the truly beautiful. His argument is leisurely and buttressed with many examples from French literary creation and criticism, but what it comes down to is the point I have been at pains to make in this section of the discussion, namely, that beauty and its concretization in art, and particularly in literary art, "seizes upon and elevates the rational nature of man," because beauty proceeds from a governed and ordered power, whereas mere "effect" or sensationalism springs from any undisciplined power.

Fr. Longhaye never reeled under the impact of a Mickey Spillane, but he would be the first critic to apply this distinction to that sort of "power"—Spillane undoubtedly has a "punch," but it is a punch that flays wildly and irrationally in all directions at once—and one of the realities it menaces is exactly the ordered hierarchy of values in any human life. Mr. Waugh, too, flays in his satire, but definitely *for* something and *against* something. Fr. Longhaye would see beauty in Waugh's work; he could discern only a negation of it in Spillane's.

This is by no means an adequate representation of the exhaustiveness with which the relationship of art and morality is treated in *Théorie des Belles-Lettres*, but it may be enough to show that the subject has been more deeply and philosophically treated than those critics think who would dismiss it as an academic and largely ecclesiastically colored debate.

To draw together the perhaps somewhat disparate threads of the thought above, let me recapitulate with a view to seeing where our argument has now led us. These various ways we have been exploring of approaching the problem of the nature of literature have established the fact, it seems, that there is an inherent moral and fundamentally religious purposiveness in literature, and that these two elements have constituted a consistent tradition throughout the history of Western literature of the basic norms for creation and criticism. Furthermore, this tradition is still operative particularly (though not exclusively) in the field of Catholic letters, which carry on the tradition in a literary world where all too frequently the moral teleology of literature is either vociferously denied or blandly ignored.

These are the elements in the discussion which, it is to be hoped, have emerged by now. A further and more practical question now engages us—namely, how can I recognize the working of these two elements? What shall I look for in my reading that will indicate their presence? Is there a hazel branch handy that will twitch at the presence of these perhaps hidden streams?

There is such a handy device, I believe. It can be summed up in one word—"inspiration." The word itself actually is unimportant; "inspiration" may smack a bit too much of partisan apologetics or of the sentimental (and materialistic) "uplift" one meets in the Horatio Alger type of book. That is not what inspiration is intended to mean here. The inspiration that the moral bent of literature implies and makes visible, as it were, is a far deeper thing. It is the sublimation, the ennobling, the strengthening of our emotional activity through the deliberate and legitimate exercise of our emotions. These, in turn, can be followed by a consequent ennobling and strengthening of character.

This quality of a good book which makes it capable of fortifying the soul has been indicated by critics down the years under many terms, as I have pointed out at length above. A recent description of the quality was given by Grant C. Knight in *The Saturday Review of Literature* (July 14, 1945), who calls it the "heroic principle." After examining many great books of the past, including the Bible and the Greek epics, and coming down to some more recent classics, the author concludes:

Our inductive reasoning leads us, therefore, to the conclusion that great literature, by donating health to mind and body, has been utilitarian and moral. We have cherished those books which have . . . kindled our wonder at our own mettle and helped to mold us into a more or less humane gregariousness.

Implicit in this conclusion is the conviction that humanity is neither imbecile nor futile, that its struggle for self-realization has meaning, and that the literature which aligns itself with this endeavor has the best chance to be remembered.

Mr. Knight is here in truly good company. His conclusion is only a modern rephrasing of similar statements by practically all the classical critics of English (and indeed any other) letters. A very handy sampling of some such classic pronouncements can be found in J. Donald Adams' *The Shape of Books to Come*. This following quotation from De Quincey is typical. Speaking of the various forms of creative literature, De Quincey says:

All alike restore to man's mind the ideals of justice, of hope, of truth, of mercy, of retribution, which else (left to the support of daily life in its realities) would languish for want of sufficient illustration . . . these ideals would often remain amongst us as mere notional forms; whereas, by the creative forces of man put forth in literature they gain a vernal life of restoration and germinate into vital activities. The commonest novel, by moving in alliance with human fears and hopes, with human instincts of wrong and right, sustains and quickens those affections.

This heroic element was obviously to be discovered in the days of the epic and of classical and Shakespearean drama. There, as we remarked earlier, was nearly always a clearly defined hero, a hero indeed with a tragic flaw, but of a stature that was noble and imposing. As literature began to take up more and more the treatment of what we in these democratic days call "the little people" or "the common man," the predominance of a single hero in a novel waned. Indeed, the trend has set so strongly against the hero of the past that in contemporary novel after novel the main character turns out to be, not a human being who has the dignity of nobility, and not a human character who has the correlative dignity of being awe-ful in his wretchedness, but a character who is merely petty. This type of sentimentally conceived character is omnipresent in the writings of such an author as Saroyan. Steinbeck leans toward this type of sentiment, and, indeed, this attitude is more or less prevalent in most novelists of naturalistic bent, whose idiom may indeed be hard-boiled, but whose characterization is usually not more than poached.

It is not snobbishness which makes us ask whether such hollow men are worth reading about. It is rather the common instincts of the human soul which may itself flinch or collapse under the real challenges life has to offer it but which nevertheless expects to find a challenge portrayed in literature.

But in the contemporary fiction that is still faithful to the cultural traditions of the past, some of the values of the hero, at least, if not his actual stature, continue to give literature what we are calling its inspirational force. Brigitte Pian of *Woman of the Pharisees*, Julia and Sebastian of *Brideshead Revisited*, the nameless little priest in *The Power and the Glory*, Sarah in *The End of the Affair*—all these are not, it is true, heroic after the measure of a Joan of Arc or a Thomas More, but they do, every one of them, have their own moment of greatness. In that moment they are noble if only in their renunciation; they thus reaffirm by their actions the heroic principle that motivates them.

The charge can be made here with some justice that this sort of heroism and the consequent quality of inspiration it may give the reader is indeed muted and in a minor key. Admitted, but let's not overlook the simple fact that most people are heroic in just that way—quietly and unostentatiously—and are not heroic all the time, but only under rather infrequent challenges. Further, the contrast even these books offer to a literature in which this heroic principle is completely lacking becomes quite evident when one compares them with such a work as *From Here to Eternity*.

4. Literature, Understanding and Charity

WE ARE now in a position to gather all the preceding discussion to a focal point which is, I believe, about the sum of what can be said on literature's supreme role. That role is simply, in the last analysis, the objective proffering to the reader of an opportunity to exercise the virtue of at least natural charity. This is not to say that the author of the book must necessarily have that goal explicitly in mind—in fact, unless he is writing as a mere propagandist and therefore abandoning his role as artist, he will *not* have it in mind. It is to say, however, that this result is something that a good book will achieve. This is the *finis operis*, and when I have closed such a book, it will require but little rethinking to discover that motives for such an exercise of charity have been deepened or, if not quite that, at least restated and reaffirmed.

A recent literary discussion turned on some points which will be of help in clarifying what is meant here by this claim that literature is an occasion of exercising the virtue of charity. One of the papers read at a recent meeting of the Institute for Religious and Social Studies at Columbia University was by Howard Mumford Jones and was titled "Literature As an Aid to Intercultural Understanding." Dr. Jones began by remarking that the whole "genteel tradition" affirms what the teaching profession assumes, and what the publishing business promises, that literature *is* a guide to intercultural understanding. The too impressionable reader, as a result, may find himself saying, without thinking too much about it, "Why, of course, it's quite obvious that the more I know about the Russians, the French, or the Chinese, the more I know about how they live and their ways of thought, the better I will understand them. And literature is one of the means I have of learning these things about them. Therefore, it's obvious that literature is a bridge to this intercultural understanding."

But Dr. Jones will go neither so fast nor so simply. He begins his demurrer by cautioning that it must be remembered that literature is but *a part* of any national or racial culture and that at the very time literature may be building this bridge of understanding, other elements (economic, political and so on) may be working just as fast and even more effectively to tear the bridge down. Further, he goes on to show, with many concrete examples, that literature has often proved a source of international misunderstanding. One concrete example which Dr. Jones does not adduce is working in this destructive fashion today. A great deal of the "literature" being exported from the shores of the United States in the shape of the more degenerate comic book and the ultrarealistic novel is causing many Europeans to believe that there is really no culture in the United States at all. An editorial in the London *Times Literary Supplement* (August 8, 1952) makes this very point and indicates its further implications in the political sphere. After remarking that "it would be unwise to dismiss as unfounded the arguments of those who contend that much of what America wishes to offer us under the disguise of culture is not only worthless but unhealthy," the editorial goes on to foresee the possibility of angry reactions which "might seriously damage the unanimity so laboriously being built up between Europe and the United States."

To go back to Dr. Jones, however, he then concludes this section of his analysis by remarking that

> . . . if literature is a real guide to intercultural understanding, the greatest literary monument of the Western world is awkward evidence. That monument is, of course, the Bible. But if any

work of literature has done more to divide mankind than the Bible, I do not know what it is; and if as a record of the culture of the Jewish people, the Bible be put in evidence as an instrument of intercultural understanding, one can only marvel at anti-Semitism. In sum, the more one studies the problem, the more baffling it becomes.

It may be observed parenthetically that Dr. Jones' difficulty about the disruptive influence of the Bible vanishes quite completely if we recall that it is not the inspired words of the Sacred text that have divided mankind, but the perverse use to which those words have been distorted by private interpretation.

To clear up the bafflement, Dr. Jones then goes on to break the problem into two aspects. He conceives that literature as a means to intercultural understanding can be studied in what he is pleased to call its "horizontal" movements, by which he means an "exchange of comprehensions among races and nations"; and in its "vertical" workings, which operate toward an "exchange within a given race or nation."

Let's consider first the second of these two movements. Dr. Jones admits, for example, that the "upper classes" nowadays know a great deal more about the "lower classes" than they did two centuries ago, and he claims that it was the great tide of humanitarian social-minded literature that has been largely responsible for this happy state of knowledge. One particular example of this broadening of knowledge that springs quite spontaneously to mind is the wide contemporary knowledge that current literature is providing of conditions among our Negro population. We have only to call to mind such books as Lillian Smith's *Strange Fruit,* Ralph Ellison's *The Invisible Man* (National Book Award fiction winner for 1952) or Carl T. Rowan's *South of Freedom* to see how this quality of "vertical" understanding prospers in today's American fiction. But the bridge that carries this type of cultural understanding ought to be a bridge busy with two-way traffic, Dr. Jones reminds us, and he wonders if literature has fostered understanding of the upper classes by the lower classes to any comparable degree. Has any large body of Negro readers, we might ask, learned anything of the upper-crust folkways pictured in Marquand?

In this sphere of literature's vertical operations, then, we must be careful not to claim too much too quickly.

What of the "horizontal" movements? Has literature stimulated to any noteworthy degree an exchange of understanding among races and nations? In this matter Dr. Jones admits that the eighteenth-century Western world

> . . . nourished a truly cosmopolitan culture operative among a literate minority in some nations . . . who were products of the same literary and philosophical system. . . . But what quality of intercultural understanding this fact exhibits is not clear. These persons and others like them were, to the extent that they participated in this cosmopolitanism, products of a single culture and not of the several national cultures to which they geographically were born.

Finally, Dr. Jones remarks rather wryly that the actual culture of any nation that reaches another nation trickles across a bridge built not by real literature, not by the finest in works of art, but rather by the subliterary popular magazines.

The whole thesis of Dr. Jones' paper is cogently and clearly set forth, and not for the sake of debunking, but simply as a caution against airy and exaggerated claims for the social function of literature. It is at the same time the type of discussion which offers a challenge to teachers and writers to clarify their own thinking and their own phraseology about the function of literature in its social consequences. Catholic professors of literature in particular should, I feel quite deeply, clarify their own thinking about the social function of Catholic letters.

This portion of our discussion, suggested by Dr. Jones' remarks, has particular relevance, it seems to me, to any Catholic interested in literature, whether as teacher, critic, writer or reader, because we now approach a point where we can, with some justification of the phrase, speak of the function of Catholic letters as an "apostolate."

This phrase, venerable and hoary as it is, is frequently bandied about with little conception of the realities that should underlie it. On the occasion of receiving an award from the Gallery of Living Catholic Authors on May 10, 1952, Jacques Maritain made some witty and wise observations on this conception of the apostolate of the pen. He began by saying that if you were to ask a writer what type of writer he was, the proper answer you should get would be: "I'm a novelist [or a poet or a philosopher or a playwright]." "But I can hardly imagine," said Mr. Maritain, "that the author would answer 'I am an apostle of the pen.' Supposing he did answer in this way, I would have very little confidence in his apostolic virtues."

We must approach a sane concept of this apostolate by realizing, in Maritain's words, that

> the immediate task and purpose of the writer is either to produce an artifact in beauty or to solve some problem according to the truth of the matter. He can and must have further aims dealing with his life and destiny as a man, but they are distant aims, which are not the operative rule and measure of the work. It is impossible for a writer who believes in God not to be concerned with the spreading of divine truth, that is to say, with the very ends of the apostolate. But this is a matter of inner inspiration which is all the more efficacious as it dwells in the secret recesses of the soul and, while quickening creative activity, maintains it in its native and genuine disinterestedness. We would risk spoiling many precious things if we let any kind of utilitarianism, even for the noblest purposes, enter the sphere of art or of speculative knowledge.

If the artist is in this wise devoted to the requirements of his art, then, Maritain continues, "he will have a good chance of being an apostle of the pen but without having any desire to inscribe his name in *Who's Who* under this heading, or to subordinate the search for truth or beauty to practical success or facility in acting on the souls of his contemporaries."

But here an odd alchemy begins to operate. If a Catholic author is thus devoted to the requirements of his métier, he will, strange to say, be reducing to actuality the efficacy of an apostolate. This springs from the simple truth, as Maritain goes on to point out, that catholic means universal. From this it follows that

> to the extent to which he is true to the type, a Catholic writer speaks to all men . . . I do not say that he will succeed in doing so. I say that he should try to. I do not mean that what he says should be of a nature to please everybody; I mean that the manner in which he says it should be such as to appeal either to the reason or to the esthetic feeling of any man who has the needed intellectual preparation.

With this corrective notion of what the apostolate of the pen really entails, let us examine Catholic letters under the aspect of their "horizontal" movement, as Dr. Jones has used this phrase above. The reasons adduced for an exchange of comprehensions among races and nations of the eighteenth century are the very reasons that make Catholic literature today a broad and much frequented bridge. If, as Dr. Jones remarks, Horace Walpole, Frederick the Great, Catherine the Great, Benjamin Franklin and Voltaire could participate in a common understanding through literature because they were products, by and large, of the same literary and philosophical systems, then Catholic literary men can today share in a large intercultural understanding for the same reason—they too, are products of a common literary and philosophical system.

We may take a further step. Not only do a Waugh, a Mauriac, a Greene, a Merton, a Hopkins, themselves overleap national boundaries and share in understanding based on the same principles, but today far more widely than in the age of Benjamin Franklin a large and growing body of Catholic readers participate in that understanding. It would seem undeniable that there is a vast field of mutual understanding which is being increasingly cultivated among Catholics of all nations through a literature that speaks to them from a truly Catholic attitude. Fifty years ago or less, it would, I am convinced, have been a rare American of Irish descent (to take but one instance) who could have stomached the very, very British atmosphere of such a novel as Waugh's *Men at Arms*. The French Catholic approach in fiction, which for long has been concerned with the psychology of sanctity, the delving into what makes saint (or sinners) tick, struck many Americans of a decade or so ago as being entirely introspective and therefore, they felt, morbid. The bluffer, more activist American attitude to this problem was too apt to consider the more tentative French approach a waste of time. But today Bernanos, Claudel, Mauriac, Bloy, are current coin in the American Catholic intellectual realm.

This international expansion, so to speak, of the boundaries of Catholic literature—and many more examples of it could be here adduced—is possible for the very reason that these authors and the expanding body of their readers have been influenced and are being influenced, perhaps to a great extent unconsciously, by the norms of a similar literary and philosophical mode of thought. On the ultimate values which these authors pose and try to restore in their works we are all in agreement. The language of sin and temptation, of grace and hope, of human struggle and divine compassion, is truly a lingua franca of the Catholic literary world both in its creative and in its creatively receptive aspects.

At the end of his magnificent critical study (*Maria Cross*, Oxford, 1952) of eight contemporary Catholic authors

145

(Waugh, Greene, Mauriac, O'Faolain, Bernanos, Claudel, Péguy and Bloy), Donat O'Donnell attempts to sum up the "community of feeling" which his extended study of the authors has revealed them to share. His conclusion is (pp. 257–58):

> Through their acceptance of the holy mysteries, of the cross, they turn what might have been—what is, perhaps, in many—a private and incommunicable suffering, into a public utterance and communion with others . . . This sense of communion . . . can ascend to a majestic and vividly present conception of the community of all mankind.

The authors, he feels, achieve this ascent because "the power of conviction which the best in these writers has over others, who are not conscious of sharing either their religious outlook or their pattern of feeling, comes, I think, from this intuitive harmony of mystery and suffering, the reverberation, even at the oblique touch of a fingernail, of the great Catholic bell."

"Mystery and suffering"—these are surely two of the dominant phrases in the lingua franca of Catholic letters. The insistence and imperiousness with which they ring throughout the work of the Catholic idealistic realists we have been considering is one of the key reasons why Catholic letters are fulfilling notably the role of speaking across the boundaries of time and nations.

On the purely literary side as well there is a common body of principles, a common approach to criticism, which is spontaneously, as it were, adhered to by Catholic authors and readers, as the three points we have been elaborating have endeavored to show.

But we may in all modesty, I believe, claim more for it than that. The argument thus far has been based rather obviously, though by no means exclusively, on a matter of quantity—a great deal of Catholic literature is being read by a great many people—but there is also the quality of this intercultural understanding which has to be reckoned with. Dr. Jones, whom we have been using so lavishly above, indeed hints at the necessity of this consideration when he concedes that "a given literature will yield to the sympathetic reader glimpses into persons and customs other than his own—that gives insight into an alien way of life." This manner of expression, however, is not a precise statement of the function of literature as a bridge to understanding. It is not precisely by revealing the alienness, the "otherness," of another way of life that literature will bridge the gap between nations and cultures—it is rather by revealing the similarities, the common interests, the common destinies, the kinship. There are, after all, two ways of considering a bridge. One may think that a bridge keeps the two banks of a river apart. The sounder consideration is that the bridge draws the two banks together.

This is the exact point where Catholic literature enters into its true function and consequent true glory. Its intrinsic purpose, the thing that it is designed to do, whether the particular author may actually have it explicitly in mind or not, is to be a channel for the deepening of charity. It may be noted that this deepening of charity can be transmuted into the exercise of the theological virtue, whose immediate object is God lovable. But certainly and more pertinently here, this charity is at least the natural charity of a rational love of one another. It is not enough for Catholic literature merely to widen "understanding" between and among peoples and nations. If with the "understanding" there does not grow at the same time a solidly motivated sympathy, consideration, respect, reverence, love, for the characters of the author's creation, and hence by extension for people in real life, then any literature will have failed and a Catholic-inspired literature will have failed most ingloriously.

But it has not fallen thus short of its function and its glory. I am convinced that any sympathetic, intelligent reader today will put down any book like *The End of the Affair*, *The Weight of the Cross*, *The Man on a Donkey*, with a deepened, more vivid realization of the frail majesty, the eternal grandeur and infinitely varied complexity and lovability of human souls. This is the way God sees human souls, and if books, even lowly novels which do not have as their first purpose the function of explicit teaching, accomplish this small co-operation with God's view and estimate of the nature He has created and adopted, then they are truly deepening the basis for and the motives of charity.

In these two aspects of Catholic literature we are close to the heart of the purposes and goals of the apostolate of the pen. We are also close to an actual realization of making literature an effective instrument in the work of cultural understanding. If Catholic literature continues to swell the numbers in every land who read more and more consciously from a common literary and philosophical approach, it will continue and widen the world of understanding that Dr. Jones praises as having been so obviously operative in the eighteenth century. If, while increasing the numbers of those who so read, it further makes understanding burgeon into love, then it will build the only bridge that can be built across the gulf of human mistrusts, suspicions and hates. This is the bridge which Christ, the Pontifex Maximus, built. On it the travelers are "neither Jew nor Greek . . . neither bond nor free . . . neither male nor female. For we are all one in Christ Jesus."

Literature can do this precise thing because, to conclude, it has of its nature a moral and religious bent which manifests itself in that particular inspiration that is the hallmark of all great books. If this inspiration consists in stirring the reader's emotion and imagination to a realization that there is some heroism in the weakest of men as well as some weakness in the most heroic of men, then the reader is playing the role of God's spy. God sees men to love them—not groundlessly, nor irrationally, or sentimentally—but because He sees His own infinite perfections mirrored in every one of them. If literature be simply true to itself, it can help bring those who approach it as it should be approached to see men in this same way. And this way is based on charity and can and ought to result in a deepening of charity.

PART IV
LITERATURE'S CHALLENGE
AND CREATIVE READING

Literature's Challenge and Creative Reading

THE PRINCIPLES we have been exploring, both the clearer principles for moral evaluation and the more intangible principles of literary teleology, carry along with them a further implication, namely that the reader, in trying to apply them, must be motivated by a desire to read in the most fruitful and satisfying fashion. He must, in other words, be trying to formulate and apply something like a philosophy of reading. This is particularly difficult and necessary in the vast field of fiction, which, because of the very fact that it is so amorphous, does not easily yield any neat and pat answer to the sensible question of how or why it ought to be read.

In searching for his philosophy of reading, the wise reader will do well to remember a most important fact—that he must keep himself open to what is too often rather presumptuously called the "challenge" of novels. This is a favorite word for blurb writers when they are describing a novel which is not a challenge at all, but rather a subversion or a debunking. Every reader is familiar with this type of book and of the character of the advertising used to promote it. It will be, let us say, a novel that deals with marriage in such a way that all religious and moral values that attach to a holy and beautiful institution are drained away, to leave nothing but disillusion, cynicism and disgust. But, sure enough, we will be told that such a book is "challenging." But we do not challenge or accept challenges from straw men. A challenge implies some equality between the contestants, and a book that seeks simply to undermine the standards of the reader is not a challenge but, as I have said, simply a subversive activity.

The fact that the word is misused, however, and therefore somewhat fallen into disrepute, is no reason for failing to realize that there is a perfectly legitimate sense in which a novel can be challenging. But it is to be feared that all too many readers (and particularly Catholic readers, for reasons that will be mentioned later), are under the impression that any novel which stirs up their thinking, gives them new insights and approaches, sets before them a puzzle without providing easily applied solutions—in a word, which challenges them—is bad because it is disturbing. The plain truth is that a little proper disturbance is often a very salutary thing.

How might one's thought be shaken up a bit by a particular novel? Let's take several specific examples and see how they can and do issue a legitimate challenge.

Here is a Catholic reader, let's say, who has heard from pulpit, radio and TV and read in the columns of the Catholic and secular press very much indeed about the matter of interracial justice, with particular reference to the place of the Negro in American life. He has heard much about the FEPC, pro and con, and he remembers that men like Ralph Bunche hold high positions in diplomatic and international life. But after all, he has not had much practical experience in working with Negroes, or for them and the justice they so often are denied. Our not too imaginary Catholic is indeed a little hazy on the whole question of justice; to him the virtue is almost exclusively confined to honesty in money matters. If you steal, it's unjust and you are held to restitution—that he knows; but that *justice* has something to do with the way others (particularly Negroes) find their place in the American social scheme of things—that looks pretty vague and somewhat romantic to him.

But then one day he comes across a book like *Cry, the Beloved Country*, by Alan Paton, or *The Invisible Man*, by Ralph Ellison, and he finds that he is disturbed. His thinking has got a shake-up. He begins to *see*, with a clarity that will be, of course, more or less vivid depending on the forcefulness of the book, that discrimination against another human simply because of the color of his skin is not merely a lapse in charity and consideration, but a sin against justice. It begins to dawn on him in a practical way that there is such a thing as *social* justice. He had known that the Popes in their great encyclicals refer to this species of justice, but the reality of it had perhaps never struck home before.

Such a reader has been challenged. The narrowness of his thinking has been presented, at least, with the opportunity to broaden and deepen. He has been given a chance to grow. He may, of course, decline the challenge and fling the book aside with the closed-mind attitude that all the hullabaloo is just so much propaganda; but if he reads the book with an unbiased mind he will realize that he has undoubtedly been enriched precisely because the book got him out of the rut of lazy thinking.

Or take another example, this time more difficult for Catholics to consider dispassionately because of their strong and beautiful realization of the sanctity of the institution involved. It is the institution of marriage, and when a book like Greene's *The End of the Affair* comes along, many a Catholic reader finds that he has been profoundly disturbed by the picturing of the adulterous affair. But once again, perhaps the disturbance was in reality a legitimate challenge. Perhaps the reader needs to come squarely face to face with the realization (the making real to himself) of the fact that not all marriages are moonlight and roses, that some marriages are stormy and wild, that others are pallid and feeble and that even the fact of the happiest marriage in the world is not of necessity a positive guarantee that all temptation has been removed to the outer reaches of the universe. If our imaginary reader rejoices in a perfect marriage, perhaps he will at least find in the story of Sarah and Bendrix in Greene's novel a picture of some of the evils he has been spared through God's grace and his own proper approach to the beauty of true marriage. Perhaps, on the other hand, if his marriage has unfortunately slipped off the track, he may see in the unhappy woman in *The End of the Affair* how human love that had been unbridled or gone sour can be brought through God's grace and in agony to be a path toward realization of the infinite beauty of the love of God.

Now, all this is not to be construed as an appeal that books written as literature set out to teach us these things. We have already dwelt on the function of literature in this matter of being didactic. But it is nevertheless true that though a good novel does not set out to teach us how to live our lives, it will, if it is a novel that has any substance at all, inevitably cause the serious reader to reflect, and, in the course of the reflecting, to question. It will, in other words, challenge.

If one does not, in this sense, question life, one is condemned to a perpetual infancy. I say "question in this sense," for there is a way of questioning, of course, which springs from cynicism and skepticism. We may ask "What is truth?" like jesting Pilate, who did not wait for an answer. But there is a sense in which we ought progressively to question our old, ingrained beliefs and opinions, and from the questions we put, to harvest continuously more fruitful answers. As we grow, our definitions of charity and justice, of our relationships to one another and to the state of which we are citizens, of our relationships to God, and so on, ought to grow wider and deeper and wiser, and the only way they will so grow is through our returning to them to ask, "What have you meant to me before and what do you mean to me now?"

There is, again, the possibility and the necessity of questioning in this way even our most sacred religious beliefs. The answers of the catechism cannot satisfy a mature mind in the way they satisfied the unfolding intellect of the child. Those answers are, of course, essentially and eternally true, and in their very simplicity (if we may use that word to describe aptly the rich and complex integralness of mysteries) they do in a way satisfy for all times and ages. But in another way, the concept of creaturehood ("God made me"), for example, ought to mean vastly more to a father and mother than to the little child who learns to repeat by rote the catechism answer. Our religious concepts must grow if we are really to grow, and very often the only way they can grow is by our putting questions to the truth that we hold most dear and most tenaciously. If we question with reverence and docility, and at the same time with a proper intellectual curiosity, we will inevitably find that the answers God gives us to hear will be gloriously rich. We must challenge even our faith, in this sense, to give up, to yield to us more and more of the riches with which God had endowed it.

In its own subsidiary way, literature is susceptible to this kind of questioning from the mature reader and at the same time offers him the challenge that will stimulate the questions.

This aspect of literature was rather strikingly discussed by the American critic, Mark Schorer, in the "Speaking of Books" column in the New York *Times* Book Review for April 27, 1952. He said, in part:

> All education, whether out in "life," or only inside schools, is a double-jointed process: up to a point, it consists almost entirely in a process of learning to accept and conform; then presently, it shifts, and it becomes a process of learning to reflect upon and to question every standard that has first been presented for acceptance and conformity. To cease to be savages, we must learn the first; to be civilized, we must learn the second.

If this statement seems at first sight somewhat suspect, I believe it will cease to sound menacing if read in view of our development above of the idea of "questioning."

As the reader learns to read with the attitude of asking so as to get rich answers, he will be opening himself to the creative aspects of literature. Literature is creative, quite obviously, from the author's side. Greene, to come back to him as our old familiar, brings to life the creatures of his conception and puts them into situations which he has contrived and which rise from the very nature of the personality with which he has endowed them. But for the reader, too, there is a creative activity which he must expend if he is to read intelligently and fruitfully.

This whole matter of the way in which the reader can grow through literature is admirably treated in *The Dynamics of Literature*, by Nathan Comfort Starr, to which I have referred before. In the first chapter, "The Creative Reader," occur these thoughtful and provocative passages (p. 2):

> In one sense literature which endures does so, not because it was once created, but because sensitive readers have recreated it again and again. This sense of participation, of cooperative effort, is absolutely essential to intelligent reading. It is imperative to feel that the work was made by a man who through the mysterious workings of talent or genius described the experiences we might have had and said the things we have probably wished to say. Only then will literature become a power.

And again:

> The reader, then, grows with and through the work; *that is, of course, if he wishes to* [emphasis added]. He sees how the words create the illusion of experience by letting his mind play upon the situation before him. He trains himself to discover how the author, through imaginative suggestion, intensifies our sense of kinship with the natural world and with other men. This does not mean simply an unthinking identification with emotional excitement. It means rather the use of emotion to give force and personal conviction to experience. The rational faculty which judges the value of things should operate simultaneously and cooperatively with the imagination to direct our attitudes to constructive ends.

I would call especial attention to this last sentence as a comment on what we have discussed above concerning the idea of the "rational pleasure" which is literature's first and formal end.

Further, from the same small but pregnant book, these ideas seem to me to buttress what we have said about the moral teleology of literature. Hear this fine passage, among others (p. 16):

The mind should not be so open . . . that ideas flow through it as easily as water through a sieve. Catholicity of taste is valueless without penetrative judgment. In works of pure diversion the reader should not confuse temporary and permanent values, he should not be misled by dissipative excitement; and works which develop ideas or seriously analyze conduct he should be able to evaluate with an active rather than a passive liberalism. This is to say that he should understand not only how well the work was done within its scope, but also how successfully the author revealed man knowing and revealing himself at his best. This best may not always be achieved, but at least the spirit that impels man to good should be a dominant force in any work that we call great.

If I may interrupt here, compare this statement with what has been said before on the "heroic principle" in literature. Mr. Starr then concludes (p. 17):

The final and highest act of criticism, then, is a synthesis, a process of concentration. After the reader has opened his mind tolerantly and flexibly to the author's breadth of information, he should then penetrate vertically to the heart of the work. And the deeper he is able to go, the more strongly he will feel that he and the author have become part of one force, part of a shaping and energizing strength.

The interesting question now poses itself. Why is it that creative reading in this sense is so rarely engaged in, even by inveterate and devoted readers? I believe I do not overstate the state of affairs. I would judge that most readers, particularly, of course, of the novel, read "just for the story," just to be entertained for an hour or two, forgetting what we have discussed above on the "instructional" role of literature, properly conceived.

Well, I cannot answer for all readers, but I firmly believe that too many Catholic readers do not read creatively precisely because they consistently misconceive the role of the critic—for practical purposes, let us say the role of the reviewer.

What is that misconception? It is that such readers want judgment on books to consist in the simple and neat statement that this book is good or bad, black or white, to be praised or damned. They want to be led, to be told that they ought or ought not read this particular book.

This is a simple approach to a complex problem, but it is not an adequate approach. The function of the critic is not to make up people's minds for them, but rather to give them the information, the tools, let us say, with which and by which they may make up their own minds. Mr. Schorer, in the article quoted above, puts this quite appositely when he says:

> Critics of literature have the same essential function as teachers of literature; this is not to direct the judgment of the audience, but to assist that audience in those disciplines of reading on which any meaningful judgment must rest.

It is quite understandable, of course, that many Catholic papers and journals, when they devote any space at all to book-review service, find themselves forced, through lack of room and perhaps lack of manpower, to confine their estimates of books to the monitory type of review. If understandable, it is nonetheless regrettable, for such reviews never will be able to give to important books the attention that is necessary if the reader is to be helped in the delicate and necessary matter of forming his own judgments in a mature way. As a foreign observer recently remarked in the matter of American films, unless there is discussion about them among intelligent and mature minds, they will be condemned to a state of perpetual infantilism. It is to be feared that much book discussion among otherwise intelligent Catholics—critics and readers—condemns all too many books to consideration on a level of infantilism.

The creative reader will approach the novel that has anything serious to offer—we are not speaking of the frothy little boy-meets-girl romance—with a certain sort of reverence, with a willingness to have his thoughts challenged in a proper way. He will come away from such a novel with some small (at least) realization that he has faced, for the time of his reading experience, the mystery that is human nature. If he has faced that, then he has grown in intellectual, and very likely in moral, stature.

This is so because, as Rev. Jean Mouroux has so beautifully said in his *The Meaning of Man* (Sheed & Ward, 1948, p. 268):

> Man is a mystery first because he is a kind of limit or horizon between two worlds. He is immersed in the flesh, but constituted by the spirit; occupied with matter, but drawn toward God; growing in time, but already breathing the air of eternity; a being of nature and of the world, but also transcending the universe in virtue of his liberty and capacity for union with God . . . But if a man is two-fold he is also one . . . [he is] susceptible of a full unity and, on the other hand, of a full disaggregation; [he] has to acquire a significance of his own, and is tossed about meanwhile in all the whirlpools of the flesh and the world. We live out this drama, we suffer from it and bleed, but remain for the most part inwardly withdrawn from it because without acute sense of it. On the day when, by some flash of intellectual enlightenment, or some effort at spiritual progress, we come to realize what we really are, we are seized with a kind of shiver. . . . Man then is radically a "mystery" that refuses to be "degraded into a problem."

If worthwhile novels are read in the creative way we have been discussing, they can and will provide that "flash of intellectual enlightenment" which is the real and only reason why the novel can claim to be an art form worth serious consideration.

CHECK
LIST OF BOOKS MENTIONED